D0443487

SWEET FREEDOM

SWEET

Freedom

A DEVOTIONAL

SARAH
PALIN

REGNERY
FAITH

Regnery Faith™ is a trademark of Salem Communications Holding Corporation; Regnery® is a registered trademark of Salem Communications Holding Corporation

Scripture taken from the Holy Bible, NEW INTERNATIONAL VERSION®, NIV® Copyright © 1973, 1978, 1984, 2011 by Biblica, Inc.® Used by permission. All rights reserved worldwide.

Cataloging-in-Publication data on file with the Library of Congress

ISBN 978-1-62157-463-7

Published in the United States by
Regnery Faith
An imprint of Regnery Publishing
A Division of Salem Media Group
300 New Jersey Ave NW
Washington, DC 20001
www.Regnery.com

Manufactured in the United States of America

10 9 8 7 6 5 4 3 2 1

Books are available in quantity for promotional or premium use. For information on discounts and terms, please visit our website: www.Regnery.com.

Distributed to the trade by
Perseus Distribution
250 West 57th Street
New York, NY 10107

CONTENTS

Introduction
ix

Devotions
1

Holiday Devotions
313

Acknowledgments
327

INTRODUCTION

It's been a heck of a year for me both personally and politically, no doubt for you, too. We all face challenges. We all are fighting some kind of battle. That's because life happens. You've sought answers that escaped amid shifting cultural sands, flighty influences, and perpetual disappointments in politicians and public policy. People ask me all the time, "I want a happy, productive life for me *and* my country, but what can we do? What is the answer?" Well, you've got the answer in your hands!

First, look back at our foundation.

Inland from the rocky shores welcoming our nation's first settlers were towering evergreen trees and white pines soaring 250 feet in the air, solidly rooted to support their enormous girth. This massive find of a healthy natural resource was better than striking gold! The evergreens would be put to good use to build and heat homes, lay trails, and build rugged ship masts for maritime shipping and a future navy.

Our Founders responsibly utilized the timber until Great Britain inexplicably passed a law that claimed the trees for the English government. When the Crown prohibited hardworking colonists from using what God had provided, resentment grew along with determination to fight for what was right. The evergreen was partially responsible for the Revolution!

George Washington commanded the Continental Army under a flag featuring an evergreen and the words "An Appeal to Heaven."

When government takes something from red-blooded patriots, it sure doesn't sit well. Our government has taken more than trees from all of us.

In my frequent travels across the country, I meet so many good people and see a familiar look in their eyes. Many Americans sense that our exceptional nation we know and love is changing so fast it might become unrecognizable. They experience a sinking feeling after watching the news, they accurately believe their religious freedom is under attack, they see government run amok, and they dread knowing that values held near and dear might soon become relics of a time gone by.

This daily devotional is about that—it's about taking action to save our country and protect freedom—but it's also about something even more important.

While many wring hands and wonder where our freedom has gone, you're going to discover that true freedom—the kind that can't be taken away—is well within our grasp. In the pages of Scripture, God gives instruction on how to live during these tumultuous times, and assures us we're here for a great purpose, for such a time as this.

Christian writer G. K. Chesterton was asked, "What is the greatest problem with the world?"

He responded simply, "I am."

Honestly, that's where the battle is fought—in the heart and mind of every one of us.

Answers to personal and political struggles can't be found in the next "great" politician, in any self-exalting self-help seminar, or in the next cultural trend. We can passionately protest, picket, and vote our way to protect constitutional freedoms, but as much as these are imperatively part of civic life, the answer to true freedom relies on a different sort of excitement. Showing you where to look in the Bible will confirm your commitment to live life well and vibrantly, and will unfold the blueprint to secure the deeply American principles of justice, faith, and freedom.

The daily devotions you'll read are "evergreen." There's no need to date every entry, because each day's Word is rooted firmly in the Old and New Testaments, the Word of God—and since He never changes you'll find the enclosed answers are forever applicable; the content is always fresh and new.

This devotional is unlike others because we're going to spend the year together dealing with real-world stuff. I'm confident that by praying for eyes to see and ears to hear, the pages will meet you where you are, and nudge us where we need to be.

My family and I have been through a lot. Surely you have too, many readers dealing with enormously more devastating trials than I could imagine. One thing I know: there is *no way* to overcome our personal and political problems with our own strength and understanding. Man is a fallen creature. We're tempted to live self-centeredly. But if we do, we'll end up doubled over by life's gut punches. I'm right there with you, certainly never setting up either myself or my family as "holier than thou." (We're really just a normal family, always banding together, no matter what…and a lot of those "whats," accurately reported or not, often unfortunately get splashed across tabloid headlines!) We recognize our profound weakness and know that our faith, certainly not our own might and power, is the only thing pulling us through trials.

But this is the secret! The advantage is: when I am weak then I am strong. Hear me on this. When we give up "self," we create a vacuum that can be filled by God's omnipotence. It means God can take every dart and arrow aimed your way, all the mocking and negative words spewed, every struggle and pitfall pushing you to the edge, every battle you never asked for but are forced to fight…and in His strength we become victorious.

The key is inside. So hang in there and don't let weariness knock you down. There's an appointed time for breakthrough; what you're going through is preparation for something greater. All the hurtful things on the periphery can stay right there—on the outside of your core being—when you focus on God and what He would have you do. Don't give up; the only surrendering we're going to do is to "let go and let God" by acknowledging our inabilities and appealing to heaven to grant the victory. Persevere!

Find your Word in this devotional for every one of your days. Before pressing in to the Scripture and commentary, ask God to guide you in applying it to your day.

Sarah Palin

MOVE PAST THE COMMA

My flesh and my heart may fail, but God is the strength of my heart and my portion forever.

Psalm 73:26

I sure don't like to fail, but here I am. When John McCain and I lost to Barack Obama and Joe Biden in 2008, it was one of the most public failures you can imagine.

As much as we fought to win that election, it was impossible to know how the nation would change and morph under the leadership of the guy who beat us. Looking back, it sometimes felt less like losing an election and more like losing a country.

Many of you might be discouraged. Often, I'm there with you: my flesh and my heart fail! But the Bible doesn't give us the option of wallowing too long. You get one comma's worth of despair before Scripture reminds us: "But God is the strength of my heart and my portion forever!"

SWEET FREEDOM IN *Action*

Today, it's time to move from the first portion of that sentence uttered by the psalmist to the next. If you are discouraged about the state of our nation, remember God is our strength! Individually and collectively. Chin up. Literally. Look to God.

Consuming the Word—Finally a Diet That Works

They are more precious than gold, than much pure gold; they are sweeter than honey, than honey from the honeycomb.

Psalm 19:10

Thank you for joining me on this journey. This hasn't been the easiest year of my very many years! So it's possible I need this as much as or more than you do. As we go through the next year together, day by day, know that dedicating yourself to praying, studying, and taking action will benefit your soul. I'm counting on that too.

In today's culture where God's Words—for example, His Ten Commandments—are literally pried off the wall to be warehoused in some dusty museum basement, it's easy to forget that we should meditate on them (Ps. 119); use them as a life tool (Heb. 4:12); and mine them for deep truths (2 Tim. 3:16–17). Psalm 19 describes God's Words as being precious, pure, sweet, valuable, and foundational for wisdom.

Sweet Freedom in *Action*

Today, invite someone to talk about how they're doing spiritually. Encourage them to eat up God's Word for the inspiration, answers, and healthy life that He intends.

WINNING THE LOTTERY

My kingdom is not of this world. If it were, my servants
would fight to prevent my arrest by the Jewish leaders. But
now my kingdom is from another place.

John 18:36

For those of us who so love this country, it's easy to forget that America is not "the promised land." Certainly, this exceptional nation was founded on religious freedom and God has abundantly blessed it. As Americans, we have enormous responsibility and a privilege that—compared to the rest of the world—is hard to calculate.

A friend said, "Being born an American is like being born with the winning lottery ticket!"

I agree with that, but still there is comfort in knowing there's more. Knowing the kingdom of God is "not of this world." I find this especially true as our federal government makes such poor decisions, wastes our hard-earned resources, and even denigrates our faith in favor of sexual "freedom" above all. (Yes, I'm talking to you, Supreme Court.)

We have been blessed, but God's reach extends much further than our nation's porous borders. He existed long before America and will exist long after. He is the Alpha, the Omega. The beginning and the end.

SWEET FREEDOM IN *Action*

Today, get involved and do something specific to help make America great, and think big about doing everything you can to fundamentally restore her. As politicians, policies, and programs come and go, real hope, and real restoration for our country, rest squarely on our relationship with God.

FORGIVE ME, FOR I HAVE SINNED
… for all have sinned and fall short of the glory of God …
Romans 3:23

Every single human being has sinned and will sin again. Darn it. I'm right there at the top having to acknowledge mine. Double darn.

I was baptized Catholic as a baby, part of a big, loyal Irish Catholic family led by our patriarch, Grandpa Clem Sheeran. Later, when I became of age to make the conscious decision to publicly testify of my walk with Christ, I was baptized in the icy waters of Little Beaver Lake. When Pastor Riley dunked me under the name of the Father, Son, and Holy Spirit, I was then lifted out of the water and…I was still the same Sarah Heath.

Yes, I'd just testified to joining the "righteousness of Christ Jesus," but I still lived in the fallen world, a world overrun by sin, which is easy to see just by looking at the news, *or* in the mirror.

No one is perfect, and in case we forget that, this verse bluntly reminds us we all need the mercy of God in the midst of our mess. And friends, with all due respect, we are a mess. Consider the example of our elected national leaders supporting a treaty with Iran that lifts sanctions against this enemy nation instead of punishing its evil acts—while still fully acknowledging that it's the top sponsor of worldwide Islamic terrorism and is hell-bent on destroying both America and Israel. Yes, we are a mess. Lord have mercy.

And what about us? It may be a hard-to-accept truth, but fallen man's nature puts us all in the same boat until we ask for the life-saving newness God offers. Accepting it is the only way to clean up the mess.

It's an important step to honestly admit that we try to excuse things in our own lives because they don't seem as bad when compared to what someone else has done. But we've got to call those things what they are: sin. Only then can we repent and be forgiven.

Sweet Freedom in *Action*

Today, examine your conscience, confess your sins, and rest in the comfort of the Lord's forgiveness.

Garden Tips for Refreshment
The law of the Lord is perfect, refreshing the soul....
Psalm 19:7

K now what needs "refreshing"? My ridiculous garden I try to grow to show kids where food comes from. I might as well just designate it the local critters' favorite feed. It's never really worked even for one big salad. I do not have a green thumb, but even I know that dead things—or things almost dead—need refreshing.

Bet you need a little refreshing or revival in your life, too. I do. This nation does. Remember those old traveling tent meetings where a visiting preacher would ask God for a "revival"? Well, don't wait for a church to put up a tent to come before God and ask to be refreshed. He'll do it right now, right where you are! When we all do this, our collective prayer for nationwide revival is answered.

The first part of the verse is even more telling: "The law of the Lord is perfect."

As our nation changes and laws fundamentally transform beyond anything our Founding Fathers imagined, it's easy to get discouraged. Even downright angry.

But God's Word proves itself as relevant today as it was thousands of years ago. It shows us not to put hope in things that man concocts. God's law—and only His law—is perfect.

Sweet Freedom in *Action*

Today, resolve not to look to government to solve your problems or give you peace. Instead, seek and receive God's revival; you'll flourish!

"This, Then, Is How You Should Pray"

*Jabez cried out to the God of Israel, "Oh, that you would
bless me and enlarge my territory! Let your hand be with me,
and keep me from harm so that I will be free from pain." And
God granted his request.*
1 Chronicles 4:10

When the bestselling book *The Prayer of Jabez* came out, people began praying the age-old prayer that Jabez uttered long ago. Immediately, as sometimes we do over anything that is popular, some Christians didn't like the fad or trend. They said it's not best to simply repeat the words that someone else prayed, and some even insisted it's "not scriptural" because God wants us to pray from the heart, rather than repeat set words.

Whatever. If your heart is in the words, there's nothing wrong with a convenient recitation. God actually gave us a prayer to repeat so He can't be against such a thing. His was the ultimate prayer to emulate—the Lord's Prayer. In Matthew, Jesus says, "This, then, is how you should pray," before going into the Lord's Prayer. That's good enough for me.

When you recite the Lord's Prayer, you're connecting to God for sure. But you're also connecting to thousands of years' worth of believers who have said the same words all over the globe in all kinds of circumstances. It's a privilege to be a part of that.

Sweet Freedom in *Action*

Today, if you haven't already, memorize the Lord's Prayer. Recite it; say it with the kids before they go to bed; even include what I have with my own family—reciting the Prayer of Jabez for good measure.

POLITICS "R" US

When the righteous thrive, the people rejoice;
when the wicked rule, the people groan.

Proverbs 29:2

On Facebook, I saw this great quote: "If you are an honest, intelligent, living citizen and think politics have nothing to do with you...you are part of the problem!" This seems to be obvious, but I sometimes hear well-meaning Christians say, "Oh, I just don't get involved in politics. The only real answer to people's problems is Jesus."

This is, of course, true. But *government matters*, and as rotten as it is, *politics matters*, because "when the wicked rule, the people groan." Under good leaders, we can rejoice, and we can lead peaceful and quiet lives or at least be led by the righteous in time of war; under bad leaders, peace and quiet are hard to come by, and strife is our constant companion even in peace.

This is obvious by a quick glance around the globe. When governments are corrupt, when they are totalitarian, the people struggle under government's oppressive weight. The Bible is not only concerned with our spiritual condition, but our mental and physical conditions as well. As Christians, we must strive politically for a government that allows people to live in peace and that requires righteous citizens and righteous leaders.

SWEET FREEDOM IN *Action*

Today, rise up! No more hunkering down, shirking civic responsibilities by being so concerned with the kingdom of heaven that you neglect your duties down here on earth. Your own town, your state, and your nation need you. Ask God to show you how to be involved for the good of our country.

AMERICA'S WAITING ON YOU, CHURCH

*...or to governors, who are sent by him to punish those who
do wrong and to commend those who do right.*

1 Peter 2:14

D o you know where the phrase "separation of church and state" comes from? If you guessed the Constitution or the Declaration of Independence, you'd be wrong. Thomas Jefferson referred to it in a letter to the Danbury Baptist Association, which had written to him seeking his help. Connecticut had an established state Congregational Church, which meant that the Baptists' religious freedom in Connecticut was not an inherent right, but a favor granted by the state. Jefferson wrote to the Baptists that he shared their belief in religious freedom, and that under the First Amendment there existed "a wall of separation" between the federal government and the churches; the federal government was not allowed to interfere with religion, an example he hoped the states would follow.

Today, it's hip to invoke "separation of church and state" to insinuate or even demand that the Church have no influence on government and no role in politics. That is exactly wrong. In fact, Jefferson's letter to the Danbury Baptists closes with an invocation of God and prayer.

I love 1 Peter 2:14 because it suggests that leaders really have to know the difference between right and wrong. Believers have a responsibility to teach and provide counsel for our government leaders.

SWEET FREEDOM IN *Action*

Today, pray for our public officials, but also hold them accountable—and tell your pastor to quit chickening out when people need to hear *truth* about right and wrong in politics.

HE CAN LEAD A HORSE, AND US, TO WATER
He leads me beside quiet waters, he refreshes my soul.
Psalm 23:2–3

Sometimes it feels like something's wrong with you if you aren't eternally optimistic. We have so many blessings here that you feel guilty if pessimism overcomes you. But even David, described as a "man after [God's] own heart" (1 Sam. 13:14), had a soul that needed God's attention.

You've probably heard the Twenty-Third Psalm countless times. But really hear for the first time this amazing truth: God *led* David's tired, thirsty soul to the water to refresh it!

The Bible is full of people who struggle with being down and out; who struggle with sadness, hopelessness, feeling insignificant. I love it because we can relate. What I love even more is: God takes those struggles seriously. He heals. He restores. He wants to lead us to reviving waters; we just have to follow!

Fellow Americans, if you need restoration of the soul, you have come to the right place. No, not to a little devotional book that I'm sitting here writing from my desk in Alaska. Instead, you're going to God.

SWEET FREEDOM IN *Action*

Today, write down the things that are discouraging you. Then, fold up that paper and give those things to God. I do it, using the paper like kindling in my fireplace on frozen winter nights. Only He can refresh and warm your soul, so quit trying to do it on your own!

Trusting God with Your Reputation
*A good name is more desirable than great riches; to be
esteemed is better than silver or gold.*
Proverbs 22:1

Funny how you can go from hero to zero in the time it takes a bull moose to charge a noisy hunter coming too close to home.

"Governor Palin is the most popular governor in the country," Senator John McCain said in 2008. I was humbled to hear campaign staff confirm to reporters I had the highest approval rating of any governor, at 86 to 90 percent.

Then, I was chosen to run for vice president.

Many of you witnessed it and stuck with me anyway through that "adventure." Some days, back then and during the continued onslaught, I asked myself, "So where do I go to get my reputation back? My family's reputation?"

Charles Spurgeon wrote, "In the matter of personal reputation we may especially be content to be quiet, and leave our vindication with the Judge of all the earth. The more we fret in this case the worse for us. Our strength is to sit still. The Lord will clear the slandered. If we look to his honour, he will see to ours."

I'm thankful I only have to rely on Christ—not my press clippings—for salvation.

Sweet Freedom in *Action*

Today, identify people who don't think well of you. (It shouldn't be hard. Their opinion probably annoys you like a tiny disruptive mosquito buzzing all night in your zipped-up tent, making it hard to rest.) If you've wronged them, ask for forgiveness. If not, ask God to remove your worry. God answers. He'll swat that mosquito away, and you will rest.

LOVE IS A VERB

*This is how we know what love is: Jesus Christ
laid down his life for us.*
1 John 3:16

O ur culture gets love all wrong, dumbing it down to cheesy greeting cards and cliché romantic comedies. Cupid is held out as the symbol for love. Personally, I find an arrow being shot through your heart by a blindfolded flying baby pretty horrifying.

Todd and I have been together since he was a pup of sixteen and I was seventeen. I can tell you from experience that if your love can be summed up in a Hallmark card, it is not going to weather life's inevitable storms.

Love may be blind, but marriage is a real eye-opener. It's not based on emotions, but is deeply rooted in action and choice. Every day, you either choose to live sacrificially or choose to live selfishly. As C. S. Lewis reminded us, love is a verb and an action. It's not a feeling.

There are days when I feel like loving Todd about as much as a bloody paper cut, and he, me…about as much as a whacked shin on a darkened staircase. Thankfully our marriage is not built on emotion. It's rooted in the sacrificial love of our Savior. Jesus showed us that truly loving someone requires great personal sacrifice. After all, His love for His bride, the Church, led Him to a painful death on a cross.

SWEET FREEDOM IN *Action*

Today, choose to surprise someone you love by sacrificing for them and doing something for them that you might not want to do but that they will love. *Show* them you love them.

TANGIBLE FAITH? UNDENIABLE PROOF!

*The heavens declare the glory of God; the skies proclaim the
work of his hands. Day after day they pour forth speech; night
after night they reveal knowledge. They have no speech, they
use no words; no sound is heard from them. Yet their voice
goes out into all the earth, their words to the ends of the world.
In the heavens God has pitched a tent for the sun. It is like
a bridegroom coming out of his chamber, like a champion
rejoicing to run his course. It rises at one end of the heavens and
makes its circuit to the other; nothing is deprived of its warmth.*

Psalm 19:1–6

I was saved at summer Bible camp surrounded by majestic mountains and refreshing waters. He opened my eyes to see Him through nature. There I realized if He could create this wondrous mountainscape, the glory of Mount McKinley, then I'd do well asking Him to shape my life—with purpose. I gave Him my life that day.

Psalm 19 is beautifully inspired poetry that beckons—implores, really—everyone to believe. "Just look up!" cries the psalmist. "The heavens declare God!" Our Master Sculptor demonstrates His handiwork. Tonight, really *see* His glorious sunset. Tomorrow look for Him in His sunrise. Day and night speak and show proof, with the seemingly endless horizon line setting a stage for the sun. It fills the whole world! There is no tongue nor tribe nor spot on earth where heavenly voices are not heard. The psalmist compares the sun to a young, optimistic bridegroom ready to embark on new life, energetic and strong. Our Maker reveals these images to every person, every day. This means we're all without excuse, as all can feel the sun's warmth, power, and magnificence.

SWEET FREEDOM IN *Action*

Today, remember that He'll strengthen your faith, too—just look up!

WORSHIP GOD FOR WHO HE IS

At this, Job got up and tore his robe and shaved his head.
Then he fell to the ground in worship and said: "Naked I
came from my mother's womb, and naked I will depart."
Job 1:20–21a

J ob provides a peek into true worship. Here he'd lost everything—his children, his servants, his livestock. You'd think Job would be utterly destroyed as a person amid all that loss, but he still worshipped God, despite his profound grief. How?

Well, worship is not about our circumstances. It is not even about what God has done. Worship is about one thing and one thing only: the fact that God *is*. *Just because He is*, He deserves our devotion—our lifted hands, our bowed knees; He is our creator and our salvation.

When we're new to the faith, we're excited when everything goes well and when "God comes through." But true worship goes deeper and often comes from tear-stained faces: if a Blue Star mom becomes a Gold Star mom, if a father loses his job, if a family is left with a ruined home after a natural disaster. Sincere and impacting worship can come from a deep place of sorrow and confusion. But that's when God's mercy shines down.

SWEET FREEDOM IN *Action*

Today, practice blessing the name of the Lord in good times and in bad. In the fullness of time, God works all things for good.

HEAR YOU ROAR

But to stop this thing from spreading any further among the people,
we must warn them to speak no longer to anyone in this name.
Acts 4:17

B efore the 2008 vice presidential debate, I contemplated the nearly
seventy million people watching that night, and I was anxious to
finally speak to important issues. The campaign warned me not to go
rogue. "Just follow the script." Eh, I knew that wouldn't work.

Beforehand, backstage, my only prayer partner was little Piper.

"Come here, honey!" I grabbed her hands and we closed our eyes.

"God, I ask you to just speak right through me tonight," I prayed. "Amen."
Piper looked up suspiciously. "Mom," she whispered, "that'd be cheating!"

Peter and John were threatened when they spoke. Their speech wasn't
the problem; it was *what* they were speaking: the name of Jesus.

Conservatives are accustomed to liberals seeking to control the conversation. When the liberals' arguments cannot withstand debate, they try
to silence "offensive" speech and attempt to make you exchange your
freedom of speech for their comfort.

But Peter and John refused comfort, choosing rather to boldly proclaim
Christ.

May we do the same.

SWEET FREEDOM IN *Action*

Today, as political correctness and pressure abound, ask God for boldness to speak. Sacrifice your own comfort to proclaim the matchless
name of Jesus. Go rogue.

A TOWER CALLED JESUS

The name of the Lord is a fortified tower; the righteous run to
it and are safe.
Proverbs 18:10

Our kids' names were chosen with purpose: Track, Bristol, Willow Bianca, Piper Indi, and Trig. "They all sound like hunting dogs," one congressman remarked. (This, coming from a politician named "Hunter"!)

I love that their names represent something deeply personal and poignant in our lives.

Names mean something. Did you know God established His name above all things? The Bible uses hundreds of names to represent Him, each bringing out an aspect of His character. Are you sick? Call out Jehovah Rapha, the Lord our Healer. Lacking anything? Cry Jehovah Jirah, our Provider. Need calm? Jehovah Shalom, our Peace.

When you run inside a tower, you are covered, safe, hidden. With all that is happening in the world today, I love the idea of running into the name of the Lord, allowing my weaknesses to be covered by His strength, absolutely blanketed by His provision and care.

SWEET FREEDOM IN  *Action*

As you go about your day, think about God as your refuge. Remember there is a place of safety and sure security where you can find answers and peace—it's in the name of the Lord! Depend on El Shaddai (God Almighty) for every need!

A NEW NAME FOR ONLY YOU

*Whoever has ears, let them hear what the Spirit says to the
churches. To the one who is victorious, I will give some of the
hidden manna. I will also give that person a white stone with a
new name written on it, known only to the one who receives it.*
Revelation 2:17

My son Track came home after his first day of kindergarten, threw
his backpack on the ground, and said, "We're changing my name
to something *normal*!" Apparently, the other kids made fun of his name,
and he wanted to fit in. "So call me 'Colt.'"

I guess "normal" is subjective.

Years later, when he was an army infantryman, top brass, cognizant
of Track's unwanted attention due to his public profile, slapped a name
patch on his uniform that read "Nunya" instead of "Palin." As in: *Nunya
business.*

It's interesting to consider how in Revelation we are promised a new,
secret name. What does that mean? Dan Allender explained, "To know
God, we must know the name God will call us. Our name is held secret
from others and even from ourself until we are in God's presence. But our
life is a long, odd, glorious journey to hear the name God will one day
speak to us."

SWEET FREEDOM IN *Action*

Let's pray that we live this odd, glorious journey called life in such a
way that God will one day call us Faithful. May we not lose hope but
press forward in doing good.

Facing Down the Political Giants

*Trust in the Lord with all your heart and lean not on your
own understanding; in all your ways submit to him, and he
will make your paths straight.*

Proverbs 3:5–6

Caleb and Joshua were men of faith, not fear. God directed Moses to send twelve spies to Canaan. Ten spies saw giants in the land and relayed fearful reports. They felt as small as grasshoppers, but Caleb and Joshua ignored the giants. With unrelenting trust, they went up at once and took possession, "for we are well able to overcome."

Every election, voters face decisions based on many reports. Ignore the media giants and consider whom God would have you support. When I was chosen to run for vice president of the United States, I prayed voters would see through the media haze to see who we, as candidates, really were. Maybe I didn't pray hard enough!

Today, many Goliaths are in our path. It's imperative we support godly, competent leaders. Just as He led Moses's men to see clearly, He'll give you the same confidence as you seek His direction.

Sweet Freedom in *Action*

Do your own homework as you consider which candidates to support. Today, ask for wisdom to make sound decisions that line up with God's will, that you won't be influenced by man's opinion but by God alone.

GODLY LEADERSHIP MAKES ALL THE DIFFERENCE
… set an example for the believers in speech, in conduct,
in love, in faith and in purity.
1 Timothy 4:12

I'm so thankful I've had the honor of serving as a mayor, as president of a conference of mayors, as a governor, as a chair or co-chair of many commissions, as a Republican vice presidential nominee. I've been at all levels of politics, and I can say this without doubt: from your house to the White House, the character of those who lead matters.

It establishes a standard for others to follow. Nadab caused Israel to sin after he followed in the footsteps of his sinful father (1 Kings 15:26). Josiah emulated David and pleased God (2 Kings 22:2). Many of our nation's problems can be solved if we elect the right person to lead. Throughout this devotional I will emphasize the importance of prayerful discernment and of taking an active role in politics. Sadly, there are some politicians who cannot be taken at their word—even some who claim to be conservative or Christian. We must carefully research candidates and hold our leaders accountable.

Be an informed voter and vote soberly and prayerfully.

SWEET FREEDOM IN *Action*

Today, pray that God will raise up leaders who will stand on His principles and put us on the right path. At work and at home, wherever you have a leadership role, work to be God's kind of leader.

A Lesson from Possum Trot

*And what does the Lord require of you? To act justly and to
love mercy and to walk humbly with your God.*

Micah 6:8

Possum Trot, Texas, is a tiny town—a former logging town.
The congregation of Bennett Chapel stepped out of their comfort
zone when Pastor W. C. Martin and his wife Donna pursued adoption, in
spite of their hectic schedules and limited finances to take on the responsibility of raising more children. Their actions sparked a movement within
their community and led to seventy-two children being placed in loving
homes, transforming their city and the lives of everyone involved.

As you can imagine, it was a challenge. "They did everything but set
the house on fire.... Actually Tyler lit up the garbage can," Martin said,
but they managed. "I never dreamed there were so many children in the
system. We're just a little church. But this problem is all of ours."

The people of Bennett Chapel are an inspiration and a model for the
nation. Martin went on to say, "The world said no to these kids. But Possum Trot said yes. And the world's a better place for it."

Sweet Freedom in

Today, reach out to parents in your community who have foster care
kids or adopted kids or special needs kids, and volunteer to make their
burden lighter in some tangible way.

GIVING FEARS TO OUR FATHER

Do not fret because of those who are evil or be envious of those who do wrong; for like the grass they will soon wither, like green plants they will soon die away.
Psalm 37:1–2

As a military mom, I know that universal fear when sending a child off to a war zone. There, where unspeakable atrocities are happening, and I would have limited communication with my son, I knew I'd need supernatural assurance to counter that natural "Mama Fear."

When it comes to our foreign policy, fear runs rampant today.

Threats from terrorists make many tremble, and their actual acts of brutality are beyond dark and evil—they're unimaginable.

For some, these are the most frightening days of their lives. Now more than ever their hope must be in the One True God. He is our security. Not knowing what tomorrow holds, we *can* know who holds tomorrow. Influence a frightened citizen today by pointing them to our Lord.

SWEET FREEDOM IN *Action*

Today, give God every fear. Fix your eyes on God and refuse to be consumed by what's going on around you. Place your trust in God alone.

Ready to Rock and Roll Your World?

Suddenly there was such a violent earthquake that the foundations of the prison were shaken. At once all the prison doors flew open, and everyone's chains came loose.

Acts 16:26

On Good Friday 1964, a giant earthquake, registering 9.2 in magnitude, cracked Alaska, setting off tsunamis and landslides, collapsing streets and buildings, and killing 139 Alaskans. It was the largest quake in our history—and we have lots of quakes. Our state has smaller earthquakes so frequently that we barely bat an eye when rumbling begins. We just hang on.

Did you know God sent an earthquake because two guys were praising Him?

Paul and Silas were exalting God while shackled in prison, bruised and beaten, not knowing their fate. Their praise caused an earthquake, breaking everyone's chains!

Praising the Lord shakes things up and sets us free. Decide with me today to lift our voices and glorify God. He'll shake up not only our own lives, but this entire nation too—and set it right.

Sweet Freedom in *Action*

Today, focus on worshipping God simply because He is Lord, no matter your circumstances. Concentrate on sensing His presence. Anticipate Him rocking your world, loosing your chains, and setting you free.

BLESS GOD, AMERICA

Blessed is the nation whose God is the Lord,
the people he chose for his inheritance.
Psalm 33:12

Between 1933 and 1981, there was only one major presidential address that included the words "God bless America."

But when Ronald Reagan kicked off his presidency by invoking God's blessing on our nation, he set a new standard. From his inauguration through President George W. Bush's final term, the phrase was used forty-nine times, and President Obama continued the practice.

Our presidents call out to God. Great! But we need some reciprocity. Our purpose is not just to be blessed by God, but to bless Him. Our Founders sought the Lord when embarking on this new experiment called America, knowing they needed Him if they were to break away from tyranny and secure freedom. It's sad how far we've wandered.

For God's favor to remain, we must turn back to Him and not squander America's blessings of life, liberty, and the pursuit of happiness. Imagine continually kicking Him out of our lives, and the life of our nation, to the point where He finally replied, "Okay, kids, I get it. You're on your own."

SWEET FREEDOM IN *Action*

Today, thank God for blessing us. Pray every heart turns to Him. Take action! Invite God back into this nation—His nation.

PRIDE VERSUS CONFIDENCE
Clap your hands, all you nations....
Psalm 47:1

When we lived in the governor's mansion, we *lived in* the governor's mansion. I had kids, so the place couldn't be a museum. We put a trampoline and swings made from fishing buoys in the back yard. In fact, my favorite memory was teaching Piper how to ride a bike there at the mansion. She was doing wobbly circles on the lawn, and I bit my lip as I watched her fall again and again.

Finally, she made it completely around the trampoline only to crash into the manicured hedges. (I believe these might be the only manicured hedges in all of Alaska.)

I ran over to her, worried that she'd be demoralized. Instead, she suddenly jumps up out of the bush, pumps her fist, and yells, "Yeah...*me!*"

Some Christians believe that it's prideful to be happy at our accomplishments. But C. S. Lewis reminds us that recognizing our own accomplishments is not pride, in the sinful sense. Pride comes only when we use our accomplishments to put someone else down. "It is the comparison that makes you proud: the pleasure of being above the rest. Once the element of competition is gone, pride is gone."

When Piper fell into the bushes, there was nothing but confidence! Joy! Accomplishment! The *good* kind of pride that I think must tickle Jesus!

SWEET FREEDOM IN *Action*

Today, allow yourself joy at what you've done and what you're doing. It pleases God!

Hollywood Influence—Rolling Down the River!

Thanks be to God, who…uses us to spread the aroma of the knowledge of him everywhere.

2 Corinthians 2:14

"Politics is downstream from pop culture," Andrew Breitbart used to say. That's exactly why my family has participated in the "pop" part of culture as well as the political portion. When Bristol competed on *Dancing with the Stars*, for example, the show received between 15.5 and 24 million viewers on *both* nights of its weekly broadcast! That's not nothing. When Republicans turn up their noses at more casual television opportunities, they are ceding cultural ground to the Left. Of course, among other shows, Palin family members have been on *Sarah Palin's Alaska* and *Stars Earn Stripes* (where Todd got to know American hero Chris Kyle).

Breitbart knew that most Americans aren't sitting around hanging on every word uttered by pundits and politicians. They have *lives*—and politics often plays only a small part in them. For some people, their only exposure to Republican politicians might be on a show about America's forty-ninth state, or with celebrities doing military maneuvers or participating in a dancing contest.

Sweet Freedom in *Action*

Today, take advantage of your current job, location, and circumstance. Be a good ambassador for your beliefs. You will do a much better job at showcasing your values than most politicians! And the good news is that the people in your environment will pay more attention to you than they will the next political debates…with longer lasting results.

POWERFUL SACRIFICE

But the king replied to Araunah, "No, I insist on paying you for it. I will not sacrifice to the Lord my God burnt offerings that cost me nothing."

2 Samuel 24:24

The enemies of Christianity think they can mock Christians by calling us hypocrites. In essence, they accuse us of not having the courage of our convictions, of not being willing to make personal sacrifices for our beliefs—in short, they accuse us of not walking the walk.

National Review writer and renowned television commentator David French is a great example of "walking the walk." A Harvard Law grad, he lamented the fact that the U.S. Army was experiencing a recruitment shortfall. Then he realized: *he* hadn't done enough to support the war effort. Even though he was a busy professional and very involved father, had to get an age waiver, and was worried that he couldn't even pass the physical, he sacrificed: he got in shape, joined the army, and was deployed to Iraq during the surge.

SWEET FREEDOM IN *Action*

We shouldn't argue for a position for which we aren't personally willing to sacrifice. I want my actions to be in harmony with my words. Today, ask God to show you what you must let go of to become a more effective witness for Christ. He'll replace it with something better as you walk the walk.

A Servant's Heart

*Jesus called them together and said, "You know that those
who are regarded as rulers of the Gentiles lord it over them,
and their high officials exercise authority over them. Not so
with you. Instead, whoever wants to become great among you
must be your servant…"*
Mark 10:42–43

I've always loved how Britain's first female prime minister, Margaret Thatcher, served England with humility and verve. "Being powerful is like being a lady," she famously said. "If you have to tell people you are, you aren't."

Jesus's life was the model of humility mixed with power. Here He was, the Son of God, and yet He led the life of a common man.

But He also warned about the "godless rulers" who "throw their weight around"—men who do not fear God, but only serve themselves. Jesus saw the corruption, hypocrisy, and power grabs of the politicians of His day—and not much has changed.

We must never allow ourselves or others to abuse positions of authority. We should be wary of politicians who enrich themselves while allegedly "serving" the people.

Sweet Freedom in *Action*

Today, search your motives. Are you following Jesus's path of humility or the path of pride? I join you in asking God to replace our arrogance and self-centeredness with a true servant's heart.

PRAY FOR POLITICIANS. PLEASE.

*I urge, then, first of all, that petitions, prayers, intercession
and thanksgiving be made for all people—for kings and all
those in authority, that we may live peaceful and quiet lives
in all godliness and holiness.*

1 Timothy 2:1–2

Yes, this applies to you. And me.

Praying for America's leaders, even when we adamantly disagree with them, might not come naturally, but God has commanded that we do it.

In our republic, there are many loud voices. Oftentimes we find ourselves shouting back at political talking heads. Yes, I know, I know. I am frequently one of those talking heads. Believe me, I hear the shouts. And believe me, I want to do the shouting!

Take this verse as a gentle reminder or an unquestionable mandate for all of us, myself included, to pray for those in authority. When we do, our hearts grow tender and we become more effective. We still might disagree, but the Holy Spirit can infuse compassion for leaders and build bridges where walls have long stood.

SWEET FREEDOM IN *Action*

Today, before blowing a gasket over a politician's preposterousness, take a moment to pray that God fills our leaders with truth, knowledge, and humbleness. I'll ask that for myself, too.

ACCEPT THE CHALLENGE; ACCEPT THE COURAGE!

God is our refuge and strength, an ever-present help in trouble.

Psalm 46:1

Gettysburg. A matchless, favorite place I've visited with family. We paid our respects and were touched when we touched the monuments and patriot graves filled with honor. In a way, you can sense the spirit there that made ordinary men do extraordinary things to make us one nation. Despite the hundred-and-fifty-year gap, you somehow feel the "mystic chords of memory" binding us to that generation whose "hearts were touched with fire."

Today, some say our nation has become so corrupt that Christians should not serve our country in the military. This is a horrible notion!

We can't leave the incomparably important duty of defending our nation solely to nonbelievers! We have an obligation—a moral obligation—to protect this country. Our freedoms are bought with blood, and Christians—above everyone else—should honor that sacrifice.

SWEET FREEDOM IN *Action*

Today, aim to influence the next generation so they never consider abdication of our defense. Help your children and grandchildren develop courage and a love of God and country.

CALLED FOR DUTY

*Therefore, I urge you, brothers and sisters, in view of God's
mercy, to offer your bodies as a living sacrifice, holy and
pleasing to God—this is your true and proper worship.*

Romans 12:1

In Kansas City it's easy to remember what really matters because they
have the National World War I Museum and the Liberty Memorial. It's
dedicated "in honor of those who served in the World War in defense of
liberty and our country."

Standing in the rain one day with my daughter reading the memorial
inscriptions was sobering and completely humbling. The reminders of
young Americans' sacrifices made a century ago in distant battlefields put
things in perspective.

Reading the center inscription resulted in tears mixed with Missouri
rain: "These have dared bear the torches of sacrifice and service. Their
bodies return to dust but their work liveth evermore. Let us strive on to do
all which may achieve and cherish a just and lasting peace among ourselves
and with all nations."

SWEET FREEDOM IN *Action*

Don't shrink back from your duties—large or small. Today, take the
opportunity to serve something greater than self.

CREATED FOR A PURPOSE

When Elizabeth heard Mary's greeting, the baby leaped in her womb, and Elizabeth was filled with the Holy Spirit.

Luke 1:41

John the Baptist leapt in his mother's womb, and I'm sure Luke—a physician—purposefully referred to him as a "baby," not a "clump of tissue" that leapt. "A person's a person no matter how small"; a baby's a baby even in utero.

Jeremiah 1:5 tells us even more about God's awareness of precious unborn children: "I knew you before I formed you in your mother's womb." Later in Jeremiah we read, "'For I know the plans I have for you,' declares the Lord, 'plans to prosper you and not to harm you, plans to give you hope and a future'" (Jer. 29:11).

When that sinks in, we realize God's omnipotence. We understand the truth that He created us for purpose; promising plans for good and not harm. Our Father does love every child and has plans for each. He has from the beginning.

SWEET FREEDOM IN *Action*

Since God knows you better than you do, He can make the call on your life evident when you ask Him. Live out that calling with courage, knowing it is good!

STANDING FOR LIFE
You shall not murder.
Exodus 20:13

In the summer of 2015, pro-life activists began releasing undercover videos of Planned Parenthood abortionists, and the country gasped in horror. Not only were the abortionists selling butchered baby parts, they were rummaging through an aborted baby's organs with a happy exclamation: "Another boy!"

The abortionist assault on children predates *Roe v. Wade.* In ancient Egypt, Pharaoh nervously noticed the Hebrews "were exceedingly fruitful; they multiplied greatly...the land was filled with them" (Exod. 1:7). The Hebrew people posed such a threat to his empire that Pharaoh ordered every baby boy to be murdered. Then hundreds of years later, King Herod was threatened by the foretelling of the coming of a Jewish king. Fearing that the king had already been born, Herod mandated national infanticide for all boys under age two. See, in both the days of Pharaoh and King Herod, God had prepared deliverers for His people, and Satan reared his ugly head in attempts to snuff them out. The enemy continues today in his quest to exterminate future generations by infiltrating culture in bizarre ways that make some believe it's perfectly fine to snuff out innocent life—to abort the most precious and promising ingredient in our mixed-up world. It is not right. It is not okay. And it's not "intolerance" to fight to protect babies.

SWEET FREEDOM IN *Action*

Today, contact your representative. If they don't have the guts to defend innocent human life, they need to resign—Democrat *or* Republican.

WHAT A WONDERFUL WORK!

*For you created my inmost being; you knit me together
in my mother's womb. I praise you because I am fearfully and
wonderfully made; your works are wonderful,
I know that full well.*

Psalm 139:13–14

When I discovered very early on that my son had an extra chromosome, that he was a boy with Down syndrome, it rocked my world. I confess, it frightened me so—I wasn't ready to discuss my pregnancy with anyone but Todd and my compassionate doctor for many months. (I got good at camouflaging my burgeoning body under layers of warm fleece in Alaska's chilly capitol. I did that for seven months!) This was in the midst of enormous responsibilities beyond my role as governor. My teenage daughter was soon to make us grandparents; my son Track was heading off to war; and my husband, Todd, was working 1,700 miles away in the oil fields. All I could do when I heard Trig's diagnosis was muster a prayer for God to prepare my heart for what was ahead.

Thankfully, my prayers were answered far beyond my shallow understanding of what true joy could be! Parents of children who aren't "perfect" in the world's eyes may face fears and extra challenges. However, our children are a blessing! The rest of the world is missing out in not knowing this.

Babies with Down syndrome frequently don't even get to draw a breath. Oh, society. Welcome children who are different instead of getting rid of those who don't match what society says is valuable or attractive.

God values the sanctity of every innocent life, no matter how small, no matter how many chromosomes. May we strive to also value these little ones. In fact, with Trig, we feel we won! My kid's got more chromosomes than your kid!

SWEET FREEDOM IN *Action*

To see others as God sees them, ask for His vision. Put your faith into action by helping those who care for our brothers and sisters with challenges.

DON'T CLOSE YOUR EYES AND POINT
I have hidden your word in my heart that I might not sin against you.
Psalm 119:11

One of the reasons people mess up nowadays? Well, they might just not know any better. In this verse, "not sinning" is directly related to hiding the Word of God—our instruction book—in your heart.

How can we know Scripture so well that it becomes a part of us and helps us avoid making a mess of things?

Probably not like this: I admit to sometimes being rushed in the mornings. Still I'm determined to read the Word before starting my day—even if it means taking the lazy way out. I close my eyes, flip the pages, point, and land on a verse, assuming *that's* the Word for the day. Then I hustle on with the tasks at hand trying to remember what I've just read. I hate to admit it, but that can be my "Bible study" MO some days! (C'mon! I know I can't be the only one!)

Of course, this is not bad *per se*, but it's certainly not the most effective way to study God's Word. There's the cautionary tale about the guy who opened his Bible for his daily inspiration with the "open and point method," and what he happened to land upon was, "And Judas went out and hung himself." The guy, realizing that was apparently not an appropriately inspirational verse, tried again. He opened the Bible to another location, where he read, "Go, thou, and do likewise."

Yeah. That. We don't want that to happen.

Sweet Freedom in *Action*

Today, I'll join you in adopting one of the many available Bible study plans. Let's give it a month and see how it enhances our perspective on life.

NOT BITTER, IT'S JUST BETTER
...not by works, so that no one can boast.
Ephesians 2:9

I'm not a perfect Christian, and—come to think of it—I've never met one. That's why I don't try to measure others' "Christian quotient." I make mistakes and sometimes don't even do a good job of explaining my faith well.

Here's the thing. I don't wish to force my beliefs down anyone's throat. Though I'll share my faith unapologetically, I implore fellow faith-filled fallible human beings to quit pretending anyone's effective in forcing others to see the light.

Only God can reveal Truth.

Let's not pretend we're holier than others. You are not. I am not. What a turnoff. We're just fortunate enough to have been knocked to our knees at some point in life and grabbed hold of the outstretched hand offering undeserved grace.

During the 2008 campaign, Barack Obama said that a lot of people in small towns are "bitter" and that they "cling to guns or religion or antipathy to people who aren't like them or anti-immigrant sentiment or anti-trade sentiment as a way to explain their frustrations."

Well, that's not me (if it's anybody). I cling to God not because I am bitter, but because there's nothing better.

SWEET FREEDOM IN *Action*

Today, try to see others as God sees them and ask for a heart that lets you love others as He does. Cling to the promises offered in Christ's nail-scarred hand. Never let go.

Righteous Indignation Can Save a Nation

He looked around at them in anger and, deeply distressed at
their stubborn hearts, said to the man, "Stretch out your hand."
He stretched it out, and his hand was completely restored.

Mark 3:5

When Jesus healed a man on the Sabbath, it was considered doing wrong—it was actually unlawful. He was angered by the reactions of the Jewish leaders, because He knew they were setting Him up and knew their hearts were stubborn. Nevertheless, He acted with compassion and healed the man's hand anyway.

I learn from Ephesians 4:26: "In your anger do not sin." Some people preach that any time your temperature rises, you are wrong because "people should never get angry, it's a sign of sin and weakness."

I beg to differ. Mark shows us that even Jesus got angry, and Ephesians suggests it's expected we'll get angry, but that anger is no excuse for sinning.

In fact, *not* being angry is sometimes a bad spot to be in. When we see abuse or manipulation or thievery or exploitation, we should feel incensed. If you don't get mad during, say, films about the Holocaust, or Planned Parenthood videos showing butchered babies, or television footage of Muslim terrorists attacking a village, then something's wrong with you. Your "anger button" is broken and needs to be repaired.

Sweet Freedom in *Action*

Remember that righteous anger is expressed in productive ways. Today, feel free to get angry at the things that anger God.

DEFINED BY SIN? THANK GOD, NO.

God made him who had no sin to be sin for us, so that in him
we might become the righteousness of God.
2 Corinthians 5:21

One of the best things about accepting Christ is that believers are called "the righteousness of God." What an honor! We don't have to define ourselves by anything else.

That means I don't define myself by accomplishments—I'm not *primarily* a wife and mother, nor *primarily* a former governor and the first female GOP candidate for vice president. Nor am I defined by failures—like, say, the first female GOP candidate for vice president to lose. I am especially grateful to not have to define myself by sin.

Rosaria Butterfield, a Christian author and speaker known for her exceptional conversion story, wrote, "Remember sin is not ever 'who you are' if you are in Christ. In Christ, you are a son or daughter of the King; you are royalty. You do battle with sin because it distorts your real identity...."

SWEET FREEDOM IN *Action*

With the Gospel, we can all have the secure privilege of finding our identities in Christ *alone*.

I (REALLY NEED TO) SURRENDER ALL
Whoever believes and is baptized will be saved,
but whoever does not believe will be condemned.
Mark 16:16

Who doesn't love the old gospel song "I Surrender All"? Though maybe many of us would prefer to sing, "I surrender some." Following Jesus is not complicated, but it does have its requirements... *everything.*

All Christians are called to sacrifice. Jesus denied Himself to the point of death! God takes *all* of our old life and makes it new.

People who suffer through struggles with, say, infidelity or inappropriate emotional attraction outside their marriage don't have a less demanding version of the Gospel. We're all in this boat together.

Married men who long for their secretary have to surrender that longing to God. Married women attracted to their kettlebell coach must resist that temptation. Unmarried couples, the Bible says, should resist their physical desire for each other outside of marriage. This teaching applies to those who have same-sex attraction too. All are invited to give that desire to God.

The requirements of following Jesus apply equally to everyone.

SWEET FREEDOM IN  *Action*

Today, try to stop seeing your own personal sin as "less than" another person's just because you're more comfortable with it. That means you're used to it—and that's not good.

Breathe In, Breathe Out; Peace

Peace I leave with you; my peace I give you. I do not give to
you as the world gives. Do not let your hearts be troubled
and do not be afraid.

John 14:27

When we don't seek God's perfect will for our lives, we aren't living with the internal safety and security God intends. We might feel burned out and burdened by our jobs. We might feel stressed out as we fail to keep up with all of the demands of modern life. This is the opposite of living in sweet freedom. Christianity, the Truth, is what sets us free; and one of the immediate blessings of accepting Christ is…ahhhh, peace.

When we're running on fumes, we're less likely to enjoy the things God has given us to relax us, like the people placed around us.

Today, reach out to your friends or neighbors. In this, I need to practice what I preach. We bought property in desert land in the lower forty-eight. (To thaw out! Well, to thaw out *and* hide out. Periodically.) I'm ashamed to say I still don't know any neighbors there. My excuse has been that I don't want their lives disrupted when we zip in and out of their state. But as I write this, I realize that's been a weak excuse.

Sweet Freedom in *Action*

Don't be afraid to get to know people, be friendly, and share the Gospel. Its blessings are meant for all, and all of us need a savior. All of us need Christ's life-changing message of peace.

The Difference between Men and Women Is No Accident

The man said, "This is now bone of my bones and flesh of my flesh; she shall be called 'woman,' for she was taken out of man."
Genesis 2:23

I hung a poster in Todd's shop: "God first created man...then...He had a better idea!"

It used to be that everyone knew the difference between Adam and Eve. Unfortunately, in the era of Caitlyn Jenner, they don't. But the differences between Adam and Eve were not accidental. And there's much more to it than Tab A and Slot B.

The Bible says it wasn't "good" for Adam to be alone. Adam and Eve complemented each other. Not only were they companions, but as the first husband and the first wife they were joined in a way that made them one and set the course for marriage and family life. Genesis 2:24 says, "That is why a man leaves his father and mother and is united to his wife, and they become one flesh."

In an era when marriage is mocked and trivialized, and believers in the biblical definition of marriage are marginalized, it's good to remember that it was divinely created for a purpose.

Sweet Freedom in *Action*

Today, if you know someone who is single, and lonely, spend some time with them. Ask them to lunch and pick up the tab!

Women's Work and Men's Work Can Be Everybody's Work
He created them male and female and blessed them. And he
named them "Mankind" when they were created.
Genesis 5:2

At home I'm constantly around commercial fishermen who curse like sailors, oil field workers with a hardcore blue-collar work ethic, tattooed soldiers with no patience for political correctness, long-haul truckers, motorheads, mechanics, hunters, and hikers. (And those are just blood relatives!) In all those Carhartts and steel-toed boots, out of all that testosterone, I don't know anyone who talks about women in the degrading way the misogynists do on TV.

I hunt, fish, plow snow, chop wood, pretend to be a jock—just like the guys. My daughters have been on the football, hockey, and wrestling teams—just like the guys. We even dress like the men at times, in warm camo hoodies and flat bills to shade the midnight sun. Our environment is rugged and real, and our Alaskan elements are a great equalizer.

On the other hand, I'm married to the most manly guy I've ever met. A famous TV producer refers to Todd as "Captain America." I've watched in appreciation as Todd stops to braid Piper's hair before a ballgame. He cooks the best salmon chowder, making sure Willow has her favorite on the stovetop when she stops by. That Iron Dog champ can change a diaper as fast as he can change the oil in one of the trucks he rebuilt by hand.

Though God made men and women so different, our talents can overlap—especially when the environment we live in demands it.

SWEET FREEDOM IN *Action*

Today, make sure your daughter knows her worth is far beyond her looks. Teach her to hit a ball or score a basket. And show your son that real men are tough enough to take on "women's work." For instance, help him make quiche. Add some venison. Real men eat it.

UNORDAINING THE ORDAINED

"Haven't you read," he replied, "that at the beginning the Creator 'made them male and female,' and said, 'For this reason a man will leave his father and mother and be united to his wife, and the two will become one flesh'?"

Matthew 19:4–5

When God created Adam and Eve as similar but oh-so-different, those very differences created the institution that's so hotly debated today: marriage.

He made us "male and female," so "for this reason a man will leave his father and mother and be united to his wife."

On June 26, 2015, five of the nine appointed Supreme Court justices voted to redefine marriage, knocking down laws all across the country. No longer, according to the court, can marriage be defined as the union of one man and one woman.

But Psalm 33:10–12 says God is ultimately in control of the nations and His plans stand firm forever, meaning everything He ordains won't be un-ordained, even by five black robes.

Franklin Graham brilliantly stated, "With all due respect to the court, it did not define marriage, and therefore is not entitled to re-define it."

No matter what happens next from the courts, and there's bound to be a "next" or many "nexts," God's law for marriage and family remains the same. And I'm sticking with His plan.

As individuals and as a society, we need to strengthen marriage, not redefine it through the courts or devalue it through sin. Do something special to strengthen your own marriage, remember that it is a union before God, and remember that the family is sometimes called "the domestic church."

PREACHERS NEED TO SPEAK THE TRUTH

For such people are not serving our Lord Christ,
but their own appetites. By smooth talk and flattery
they deceive the minds of naive people.
Romans 16:18

Too many people in the faith-filled community fear persecution, and so want to keep a low profile. But I've got a newsflash for you: if you're not ticking someone off, you're not doing your job. We're talking about the future of our free republic. Whether we want to be in it or not, we're in a cultural and political war for the future of this country, and Christians are on the front lines.

Pastors have a special responsibility to step up and feed the flock with the Word that strengthens. If they don't, they're wasting everyone's time— worse, they're misguiding people.

So here's my message to pastors: ask God to give you the courage to speak the Truth.

If you do, congregations will give you respect! America will give you thanks! We've got your back!

SWEET FREEDOM IN *Action*

Tell your pastor you don't want "smooth talk and flattery"; you want the honest Gospel Truth.

Raise the Roof

When Jesus saw their faith, he said to the paralyzed man,
"Son, your sins are forgiven."
Mark 2:5

F aith can heal; but faith needs to be combined with effort.

"Forget it," the paralyzed man could've said in the book of Mark. "Too much work." His only chance at healing was getting to Jesus, but a dense crowd blocked him. He could have told his friends who carried him to just turn back. But desperate times call for desperate measures. Pointing toward the roof, maybe he demanded, "C'mon guys, get me up there!" They ripped a hole in the roof so the paralytic could be lowered down to Jesus. Jesus called their action *faith,* faith in action, and a paralytic was healed!

It's easy to get discouraged today, but God is looking for those with guts and gumption to find answers in Him!

Getting lost in the crowd, going with the flow (only dead fish do that), won't cut it.

Sweet Freedom in *Action*

Today, try to reach God as if your life depends on it. Because it does. Ask God to give you strength to find a way beyond the crowd to find Him.

IT IS THE BEST OF NEWS, THE WORST OF NEWS

We also know that the law is made not for the righteous but for lawbreakers and rebels, the ungodly and sinful, the unholy and irreligious, for those who kill their fathers or mothers, for murderers, for the sexually immoral, for those practicing homosexuality, for slave traders and liars and perjurers—and for whatever else is contrary to the sound doctrine.
1 Timothy 1:9–10

There is a pastor who says, "Before you hear the good news of the gospel, you first have to hear the bad news."

Here's the bad news. Though many Christian pastors try to soften teachings, the Bible condemns sex outside of marriage. But the "bad news" gets even tougher: the Bible condemns *all* sexual activity outside of anything but heterosexual marriage.

The bad news, in other words, is that condoning today's societal changes regarding marriage is worse than we thought. The good news? God is good, all the time; He's better and more forgiving than earthly minds can imagine.

SWEET FREEDOM IN *Action*

Today, let's assess ourselves honestly. Do we participate in wrong things? This question runs the gamut, I know. Assess, then just talk to God about it. Ask for understanding of His life-changing message in the Word.

PRACTICE YOUR FAITH—WHATEVER THE COST

We are hard pressed on every side, but not crushed; perplexed,
but not in despair; persecuted, but not abandoned; struck
down, but not destroyed.

2 Corinthians 4:8–9

The stories seem endless. Christian bakers being fined, wedding photographers being prosecuted, even Christian owners of a pizza shop being threatened—all in the name of unconstitutional "sexual rights" that allegedly trump our actual constitutional rights to free speech, the free practice of our religion, and freedom of association.

Since when is it right to force people to violate their religious beliefs and to participate in ceremonies that they deem sinful? This is America, people. And faith-filled Americans need to stand up and be counted. Religious freedom is our constitutional right—and we should be allowed to practice that freedom every day, everywhere.

And if we are persecuted for that—so be it. We must practice our faith whatever the cost. And we must trust that our fellow Americans will join us to defend our sacred rights.

SWEET FREEDOM IN *Action*

Today, I challenge you to fight for what is right; fight to restore our religious freedoms. I believe the battle will be won...little by little...person by person...wedding cake by wedding cake.

Mom's Right: More Honey, Less Vinegar

*Now that you have purified yourselves by obeying the truth
so that you have sincere love for each other, love one another
deeply, from the heart.*
1 Peter 1:22

I often think that "social media" is anything but. Have you noticed that rather than actually bringing people together in a fruitful way, it often leads to bullying and recriminations and senseless arguments?

I've about had it up to here with social media, but I have to acknowledge it's here to stay, in some form, so let's rethink reactions that are becoming habitual. Before "unfriending" someone, take a second. Why did God put that person in your life...or at least on your social media feed?

With all the acrimony between liberals and conservatives over issues like immigration law and order, welfare reform, many social issues, and everything else...well, it's easy to become isolated in our stance on biblical truths.

Sweet Freedom in *Action*

Try this: do something kind for your liberal neighbor today. See if doors open with a sincere offer of hospitality. Hold the vinegar, and bring the honey of Christian charity and love.

SLAPPED WITH THE RACISM LABEL? WELL, PEEL IT OFF!

There is neither Jew nor Gentile, neither slave nor free, nor is there male and female, for you are all one in Christ Jesus.
Galatians 3:28

Todd is an Alaskan native and part Eskimo; my kids' Yupik Eskimo heritage is a badge of honor, not a chip on their shoulder.

You'll not see my kids falsely charging someone with racism just because they disagree with an opinion.

But liberals slap that racist label on me—and any other conservative—simply to stop debate on any issue. What a tactic! It immediately puts you on the defensive.

Racial tensions are mounting, and Americans are being divided. We don't have "whites only" water fountains or "separate but equal" schools anymore, but, ironically, race relations in this country seemed to take a giant step backward under the presidency of Barack Obama.

Slogans proclaiming "black lives matter" have clouded the truth that *all lives matter*. And, to show how crazy things are, both a college president and a Democrat politician have actually apologized for saying that "all lives matter," as if that were somehow wrong.

But the fact is, we're all created in God's image.

SWEET FREEDOM IN *Action*

Today, pray against the spirits of division and deception that are at work in the media and the culture. Support leaders seeking to unite America rather than divide us for presumed political gain.

THROW RACIAL DIVIDE BY THE WAYSIDE
*But let justice roll on like a river, righteousness like
a never-failing stream!*
Amos 5:24

It's funny that today a lot of liberals like to pose as champions of civil rights—but also want to keep religion out of politics.

Yet it was religion that helped America overcome racial divisions in the past.

It was an ordained minister, and a civil rights movement full of ministers, that eventually did away with segregation and guaranteed true equality for all Americans.

During these contentious times, it's good to reflect on the life and legacy of Dr. Martin Luther King Jr., who dedicated himself, as a Christian pastor, to peaceful change in pursuit of justice.

With Dr. King's faith in God, his respect for life, and his unwavering hope in a brighter, stronger future, let us recommit to continuing his work for a more peaceful and just nation.

"Our lives begin to end the day we become silent about things that matter," he said.

SWEET FREEDOM IN *Action*

Today, with so many seeking to sow division, especially racial division, let us find opportunities to show love and respect for one another. Our unity as a nation under God is what will keep our republic standing.

LIKE THE GPS STEERING YOU WRONG ON A FAMILIAR ROUTE
*You, Lord, hear the desire of the afflicted; you encourage
them, and you listen to their cry....*
Psalm 10:17

It cracks me up when we're busying around the house in the morning before school and someone's choosing their outdoor gear, asking, "Anyone know what the weather is today?" We're standing by the door, looking out the window, but still you'll see heads bow and thumbs tap to find a weather app on our phones...so we can see what it's doing outside. There are times when it might be sunny outside but the speediest Googler looks up and confidently says, "It's snowing. Wear a parka."

Relying on faulty information. Especially when we have access to the truth. What the heck are we thinking?

I guess that's the point. A lot of us go through life without actually thinking, without seeing what's really going on around us. We rely on messages from the culture (or from Google), and we go along with the crowd. That's an easy way to get lost in a spiritual wilderness.

"Keep the Faith!" isn't a platitude I like to write below my autograph. Keeping the faith is the hard work of the Gospel. When we're lost, God whispers through His written Word, "Trust in the Lord with all your heart.... Lean not on your own understanding..." Our own understanding just doesn't cut it, especially when we have access to true wisdom. Trust in God.

SWEET FREEDOM IN *Action*

Today, resolve not to be guided by the drift of popular culture or questionable information from the mass media, but turn to God, who never fails to strengthen and comfort.

SHOULD YOU VOTE FOR THE "CHRISTIAN-Y-IST" CANDIDATE?

Then the king placed Daniel in a high position and lavished
many gifts on him. He made him ruler over the entire province
of Babylon and placed him in charge of all its wise men.
Moreover, at Daniel's request the king appointed Shadrach,
Meshach and Abednego administrators over the province of
Babylon, while Daniel himself remained at the royal court.

Daniel 2:48–49

Somehow over the past few decades, Christians have gotten it into their heads that they should vote for the most "Christian" candidate. Actually, that's not good enough.

Here's a thought experiment. What if you had the choice to vote for either a Baptist Sunday school teacher or a divorced Hollywood actor? This really isn't a thought experiment; this was the real choice Americans faced in 1980. Many evangelicals rightly voted for Ronald Reagan over Jimmy Carter because they figured Reagan would represent their virtues more than the peanut farmer who taught Sunday school on the side. They were right.

In the Bible, the leaders God chooses to advance His purpose are a diverse bunch, and none of them is perfect. In the Old Testament, God even used Babylon's King Nebuchadnezzar to protect and promote Daniel and his Jewish friends to important, influential positions over the city.

SWEET FREEDOM IN *Action*

Today, I advise you not to judge politicians based on religious doctrine, but on values, dedication, and performance. And when you find them, roll up your sleeves, get to work, and get them elected.

SWEAT: SHUSH, IT'S SANITY

For physical training is of some value, but godliness has value for all things, holding promise for both the present life and the life to come.
1 Timothy 4:8

After having my fourth child, I ran a sub-four marathon. That's plod-along talk for racing 26.2 miles in less than four hours. Okay, I sprinted in under the wire, literally, to make 3:59, but it hurt like hades so I was just happy to finish. I couldn't duplicate that effort today if all my low-carb ketosis-inducing pounds of protein depended on it.

Running up north isn't easy. Some days, you have no idea how much I dread lacing up cleated shoes to shuffle down an icy road. Shoot, even in summertime I don't have to look hard for reasons to die in that first mile out. However, sweat is my sanity.

This verse references godliness, but don't skip over the importance of taking care of your physical self. It is prudent to tend to both spiritual and physical health. Though exercise is not as profitable as devotion to faith, it has its place. God has work for us. To do it, we need to take care of our "earthly temples." Ignoring the need to put down the fork and move means missing out on God's best plan for you.

SWEET FREEDOM IN  *Action*

In contemplating today's devotion, that's enough! Don't think—just do. This body is the only one you'll ever have. You're not the only one who'll periodically feign enjoyment of sweat and gasping breath. I'm right there with you. As the slogan on my (admittedly impolite) marathon shirt had it: Shut Up and Run.

TRUE HOPE, REAL CHANGE

For God so loved the world that he gave his one and only Son,
that whoever believes in him shall not perish but have eternal life.

John 3:16

Remember seeing this verse everywhere? Placards at baseball games, spray-painted on bridges, biceps tatted up with John 3:16. It's probably the most beloved and memorized verse because it sums it all up—the hopeful miracle that the world can find in Christ.

But doesn't it indicate that Christ died? Yes, but this isn't cause for despair. How counterintuitive that the story of Christ's death also holds the triumph of hope over pain and sorrow! Hope is a Christian virtue, but it's also a deeply patriotic virtue. Hope makes us dream and achieve the seemingly impossible, and we're free to succeed in America!

Hope is who we are individually and as a nation. It's why we can believe that our best days are yet to come. Our hope is far from naïve or baseless: Christ's resurrection proves we have every right to be hopeful. Accepting God's gift of His beloved Son is our solid foundation.

SWEET FREEDOM IN *Action*

Ignore a cynical worldview that declares all is lost. Change that! Keep hoping, keep working for a better future. Ask God to release you from despair and fill you with faith in His goodness.

IT'S GO TIME

There is a time for everything, and a season for every activity
under the heavens: a time to be born and a time to die...
Ecclesiastes 3:1–2

Living in the "Last Frontier" is full of fun adventure and rugged terrain...and also increased risk of injury. While some people think twice
before jumping in an airplane you just rolled out of your garage, the enormous size of our state means it's no big deal to hop in a puddle jumper to do
chores. (We put our kids on planes just to get them to soccer games.) Even
running out to get the mail means dodging a moose or two along the way.

"Hey, when it's time to go it's time to go," we frequently say around
the house. It may sound macabre, but it's not. It's truth. God's timing is
His own.

Piper hasn't discerned that people outside our family may not appreciate
our candid deference to God's sovereignty. Obsessed with getting her learn-
er's permit, she practiced endless vehicular touch-n-gos up and down the
driveway. One day, Todd's buddies had congregated at the end of the drive
in front of his shop, paying no attention to the little girl in the big black truck.

"Slow down," I hollered. "You're going to kill them all."

She just rolled her eyes and sighed, "Eh. When it's time to go..."

SWEET FREEDOM IN *Action*

Today, remember that God's timing is perfect. "Let go and let God"
doesn't have to be cliché; it works better than trying to orchestrate your
own timeline.

BUSTING OUT WITH LIFE!
Do not boast about tomorrow, for you do not know
what a day may bring.
Proverbs 27:1

Race car great Mario Andretti said, "If everything's under control, you're going too slow." We have two summertime speeds: fast and faster. The Land of the Midnight Sun gives us such short, sweet warmer months that we try to cram it all in before the leaves change and snow flies again. Such rapid change warns us we'd better be full-speed ahead to capture every minute in the great outdoors.

Maybe those living in the lower forty-eight find it intriguing, the way we view seasons and respond to the ever-changing natural world.

The Bible teaches us that God alone knows what our future holds. Instead of putting off that thing that you've wanted to do your whole life, why not put it into action now?

Right now is the only time you know you have. The present *is* a present, so use it. Get up, soak it up, enjoy every minute of it.

SWEET FREEDOM IN *Action*

Today, go forth. Let's stop procrastinating and stop taking time for granted. Make today useful for God's glory and purpose.

Fruitful Golden Years
They will still bear fruit in old age, they will stay fresh and green...
Psalm 92:14

We're blessed to have five generations of family around, learning, living, loving together. Todd's grandmother, a beautiful Eskimo elder, still speaks Yupik and weaves intricate baskets using grass, wood, fur, porcupine needles, and other bits of nature. Lena, who is ninety-five years old as I write, was a hardy commercial fisherman in Bristol Bay, setting nets from handmade wooden boats powered on rough waters by only the wind, the tides, and very strong hands.

My in-laws' store sits on 2nd Avenue in Dillingham, proudly serving the robust fishing community. Every spring the hardware section bustles with activity, the town acting as a hub for surrounding villages preparing for upcoming salmon runs. One summer Bristol and Willow worked there together (pro bono, I hope, based on reports of their horseplay) only to get "fired" together, by their grandmother! Nepotism schmepotism. It's inspirational to see how God has used—and is using—Lena to faithfully teach the hard lessons of love, life, and commerce to family and her Alaskan community.

Sweet Freedom in *Action*

Today, be faithful to your calling and community. Don't let past wrongs or regrets build in your soul so it can remain free for the Holy Spirit's filling.

UNPLUGGED

One thing I ask from the Lord, this only do I seek: that I may dwell in the house of the Lord all the days of my life, to gaze on the beauty of the Lord and to seek him in his temple.

Psalm 27:4

According to researchers whom I believe, the smartphone has eaten away our attention spans. In 2000, our attention span was twelve seconds. Now, it's down to eight. As a comparison, goldfish are believed to have an attention span of nine seconds. (Just because I believe the research doesn't mean I won't ask: "Huh?! How can you tell? And what do goldfish have to think about?")

The point is, technology is waging a constant battle for your attention. All those gadgets charging up on the kitchen counter are a blessing and a curse.

King David surely had lots of folks with lots of "asks" calling on him day and night. Yet he penned from his heart that there was only one thing he focused on above all else—gazing at the beauty of the Lord. In the midst of the swirl, I often have to take a deep breath to center on the most important thing—Jesus.

SWEET FREEDOM IN *Action*

A practical way to center is to unplug all the white noise humming around you and put on worship tunes. I memorized most of my verses growing up listening to Mom's old Maranatha records! In that place, ask the Holy Spirit to fill you with desire to spend more time focusing on God. Okay, reading Scripture on your Bible app is acceptable.

GIVE THAT PRODIGAL KID TO GOD
I will extol the Lord at all times; his praise
will always be on my lips....
Psalm 34:1

Are you the parent of a prodigal? Is your heart heavy watching your beloved child veer off into a culture that prefers to sweep God under the rug? You look back to better days, when you were cradling your sweet, innocent newborn. You might wonder, *what went wrong?* Well, don't be dismayed. Remember God's promises! When you let go of a grown child to let them make their own decisions, you might feel powerless and you might cry out to heaven in fear and worry.

But thanks be to God! When our praises go up, the blessings come down. Study His promises! Know why praise can continually be in our mouth, despite any circumstances. Your situation will turn out right.

However our parents raised us, at the end of the day, we and our cherished children have to learn some things on our own. No one can live our lives for us. We have to do it.

You have raised your children for sweet freedom. Pray that they use their freedom to get wiser and stronger.

They will come back. Plan for that celebration.

SWEET FREEDOM IN *Action*

Today, remember that the thoughts God has toward you and your loved ones are of good and not evil. No matter how it looks right now, you can lean on God. Trust Him.

THE JOY OF GIVING

*Each of you should give what you have decided
in your heart to give, not reluctantly or under compulsion,
for God loves a cheerful giver.*
2 Corinthians 9:7

Growing up, I was taught that the Bible says we can "test" God in our tithes and offerings. Without fail, He always repays when we give. It's been fun to pass that lesson on to my kids because they clearly see the proof.

The blessing of giving is participating in it willingly—cheerfully even. Our government has it backward. Politicians put their hands in someone else's pocket instead of treating other people's hard-earned money as they would their own. In Washington, there's too much addiction to OPM (other people's money). In fact, when politicians' personal finances have to be disclosed when they run for office, some of the most self-described compassionate liberals are revealed as the least charitable.

That's not God's plan. He's calling *us* to step up. The easy way out is to simply depend on the government to hand out everything, but the first lesson in any good Econ 101 course is: "There ain't no such thing as a free lunch." Our government was never intended to rob from Peter to give to Paul. Safety nets? Yes. Unnecessary government dependency? No. Joy, blessings, and productivity are found in *voluntary* giving, in *personally* providing help to the needy.

SWEET FREEDOM IN *Action*

Today, give something extravagant to God, not out of guilt or obligation, but because you delight in God's generosity and want to emulate it!

MIDNIGHT PRAISE

*About midnight Paul and Silas were praying and singing
hymns to God, and the other prisoners were listening to them.*
Acts 16:25

My home state is called the Land of the Midnight Sun because the ball of fire essentially never sets during the summer months. This means we dare not tell our kids to come home before dark or we won't see them until autumn.

I like the book of Acts pointing out Paul and Silas praying at midnight.

These men were discouraged, and with good reason to be. Locked up for obeying God, they could have sunk down in their cell and shouted to the heavens, "So this is what preaching Christ gets us!" It was midnight in their lives, very dim indeed.

Instead, they praised God!

Do you know what happens when you praise Him? It's inviting Him closer. But is it easy to do in discouraging times?

Absolutely not.

Yet He is worthy, and no matter how dark the day or night appears, He proves this.

SWEET FREEDOM IN *Action*

Read passages today that make you realize you were created to worship. Remember He is worthy of praise and adoration not just in the good times, but even more in your midnight hour.

KILLING WITH KINDNESS? I'LL TAKE THAT.

Be kind and compassionate to one another, forgiving each other, just as in Christ God forgave you.

Ephesians 4:32

There was a season in the Palin world when a strange author moved in right next door. He was a pretty famous guy in the book world, so people paid attention when he announced he'd moved all the way from New York to write a book about us. This wasn't a shining season. Todd had to build a huge fence to separate the guy from practically being able to touch the kids when they played in the yard. It worked. Todd's fence was more effective than our country's nonexistent one along the border. But then the new neighbor resorted to standing high on his porch with binoculars to see what he could see. Thank God it only lasted a year and a half; then I could finally open my west-facing curtains again. His mission to "keep an eye on us" was complete for his hit-job book.

He was out for himself.

Everyone seems basically out for themselves. In my line of work I see it every day. If you don't agree with someone's view, they often pull out all the stops to condemn you. It's brutal! I know it's hard to understand the concept of forgiving someone who doesn't want it, because they'd just as soon double up their efforts to insult.

I admit it: sometimes, my first reaction is retaliation. But we're told to forgive. Even further, the Bible says to help our enemies! God tells us that vengeance is His, not ours. We need to leave that to God, because He is the true and final judge.

SWEET FREEDOM IN *Action*

If someone is trying to destroy your reputation today, force yourself to let go of what you can't control, which is what other people say and think about you. God's got this covered in the fullness of His time. Our role is to "kill them with kindness," as the old saying goes. I'll take that.

Forgiving the Unforgivable

Jesus said, "Father, forgive them, for they do not know what they are doing." And they divided up his clothes by casting lots.

Luke 23:34

At the court hearing after the horrific shooting inside the African American church in Charleston, South Carolina, the families of the murdered spoke directly to the gunman...one at a time.

"I forgive you," said a woman whose mother was killed in cold blood. The shooter didn't respond. He stood, motionless. Even as the agony of their loss was evident through sobs, the victims' families told the criminal they were praying for him.

It's one thing to forgive someone who has asked for forgiveness. It's another thing when someone hasn't acknowledged wrongdoing and you forgive them anyway. These South Carolinians demonstrated the forgiveness of Christ so beautifully that a nation held its breath.

Jesus was innocent hanging on the cross as His oppressors abused, mocked, and tortured Him. Nonetheless, He asked His Father to forgive them, even though they hadn't requested it or acknowledged their horrid offense. How do we wrap our minds around that, much less emulate it?

Thank you to the families in Charleston for giving us a poignant example.

Sweet Freedom in *Action*

Today, look to the people of Charleston. Try to forgive offenders even if they haven't asked, but know that God understands if you can't demonstrate that kind of forgiveness on your own. He wants you to receive His grace so with Him you can forgive those who hurt you or your loved ones.

Unexpected Episode? Meet Enduring Faith.

Blessed is the one who perseveres under trial because, having stood the test, that person will receive the crown of life that the Lord has promised to those who love him.

James 1:12

"Mom, you gotta get that checked out," said Bristol, an aesthetician who's worked for years in a wonderful Anchorage dermatology office.

"What?" I shrugged her off, looking at the thing she'd spotted on my leg. I don't do doctors. If I can help it.

"That!" she insisted. "That weird thing."

I refused. She insisted. I relented, and the biopsy came back: squamous cell carcinoma. Cancer. A surgeon dug it out; he got it all. No big deal.

"So call me a cancer survivor, eh?" I jokingly asked Bristol, feeling silly since my brush with the disease was so slight as others suffer enormously. Nope, instead she bought me a coffee mug with a survivor ribbon on it and called it good.

God can calm your thoughts and give you rest when life happens and the unexpected puts a wrinkle in your plans. I didn't have to suffer sleepless nights or wonder how it was all going to work out, though that episode added to that year's being another "year of the unexpected" that was pretty hard to believe. That's part of the deal and just one of the benefits of giving your life to Christ.

You've nothing to lose and eternity to gain by receiving Him now. Ask Him to forgive your sins and come into your life; pick up the Word; and tonight put your head on your pillow while God's presence renews you. Then, like me, may you wake up to a ribbon 'round your coffee cup, reminding you: He's got this.

KNOW THE ENEMY TO DEFEAT THE ENEMY

...the face of the Lord is against those who do evil, to blot out their name from the earth.

Psalm 34:16

L ast fall on a peaceful Sunday afternoon, Bristol was returning home with Tripp when she sensed something was wrong. Someone was waiting for her on her front steps.

The stranger said he'd been waiting; he told Bristol he wanted her time.

She knew immediately this was a stalker who'd sent thousands of bizarre, threatening messages to her through Facebook and other means. Even after she'd blocked him, he'd assume different identities, delusionally insisting he worked for me and had a relationship with Willow, and he ramped up his dangerous harassment of Bristol. When she realized this guy had come all the way from Florida to Alaska for some kind of encounter, she grabbed Tripp and ran for help. We'd been through this before. This particular stalker ended up in jail, and there are others in or out of jail today who've stalked our family. They're messed up men used by the enemy to commit acts of evil.

One may nonchalantly take the above Scripture figuratively until something bad happens. Then you understand how God preserves your life. We've had many disturbing, even dangerous moments since my family was thrust into the spotlight in 2008. This past year was particularly trying. For us it's been imperative that we remember God is greater than the enemy of our soul. He's more powerful, and His omnipotence holds our destinies. I cannot fathom how it would be not to have this promise to cling to. I pray for everyone reading this devotional that whatever threats they might face, their faith will pull them through.

SWEET FREEDOM IN *Action*

I pray for you now, that God's hand of protection shields you from those who wish you harm.

Good Hair Day
And even the very hairs of your head are all numbered.
Matthew 10:30

Chinese-American evangelist Bob Fu tells the true story of a man in the Chinese countryside who was sent to a labor camp because he ran a "house church." When the man lined up with the other prisoners to get his head shaved, he noticed his crying daughter through the gate. She knew a shaved head would mark him as a criminal…regardless of the fact that he had done no wrong.

"Remember what the Bible says?" he comforted her. "Every piece of hair is counted. Without His permission not a single piece can fall to the ground."

When the guard got to him, the clippers mysteriously stopped. The guard examined them, got them working, and placed them back on the man's head. Another malfunction. Another guard hastily marched over with his own set of clippers. They broke too.

"There must be something wrong with your hair!" the guard yelled angrily, sending him away. As the man left, the guard's clippers began buzzing.

Sweet Freedom in *Action*

Today, remember that miracles still happen, that God protects His followers, and that He is in control of your destiny.

CITIZEN JOURNALISM SCHOOLS THE BIG DOGS
*How beautiful on the mountains are the feet of those who
bring good news... Your watchmen lift up their voices;
together they shout for joy.*
Isaiah 52:7–8

I graduated from the University of Idaho with a degree in journalism. Though I value what I learned in college, it's invigorating to see that the Internet has put the power of a reporter in the hands of everyone. So-called "pajama journalists"—concerned citizens—have broken stories, broken through the silence of the mainstream media, and even exposed bad reporting from the alleged professionals.

The Internet can be a great tool for reporting good news, bringing good tidings, and exposing injustice.

A lot of people in politics don't want to tell it like it really is. Neither do a lot of people in the big-dog media.

But just as the invention of the printing press made the Bible available to everyone who could read, so the Internet has put the power of the press into the hands of each and every one of us.

SWEET FREEDOM IN *Action*

Today, take advantage of this great gift and communicate the good news about God, and about America, and do your part to contribute to the next Great Awakening.

GOD'S MENU

*…God created to be received with thanksgiving by those who believe
and who know the truth. For everything God created is good,
and nothing is to be rejected if it is received with thanksgiving.…*
1 Timothy 4:3–4

I should go into the refrigerator magnet–making business because I've got great one-liners that everyone should see before opening the fridge door:

I eat, therefore I hunt.

I feed my family healthy organic protein, I just have to shoot it first.

My meals come wrapped in fur, not cellophane.

God provided in His creation everything we need to be sustained, obviously including food. That's why many of us hunt: to utilize the food supply that is good and to be received with a grateful heart. It's all a part of His creation that takes care of us. It's our responsibility and privilege to reciprocate by taking care of it.

God put man at the center of creation. We are to be good stewards of the environment. People are not an environmental problem. They are created in God's image. They are, ultimately, in their ingenuity, their creativity, their compassion, the answer to environmental problems. The world is meant to belong to man, not mosquitos. And there is absolutely nothing wrong with feasting on the bounty God has provided us.

SWEET FREEDOM IN *Action*

Take time today to thank God for all His nourishing blessings. Teach your kids about the food chain and the natural cycle of life on this ever-changing planet. Really instill in them an appreciation for nature by getting out in it with them!

FRIENDS AND ALLIES

Two are better than one, because they have a good return
for their labor: If either of them falls down, one can help
the other up.

Ecclesiastes 4:9–10a

Israel, special to God, is also special to the United States.

In 2011, Todd and I had the honor of visiting Israel and enjoying a private dinner with Prime Minister Benjamin Netanyahu and his wife, Sara, on Purim no less! What a rare privilege for us, private citizens, to sit down with not only a head of state, but a hero so protective of his country that we'd all do well to learn from him and absorb his strength.

That evening, we talked about how Mordechai sent his courageous Jewish cousin Esther to risk her life by approaching the king and asking for protection for her people.

With Israel's neighbors vowing to wipe her off the map, she looks to the United States to stand alongside her. We must elect leaders who will honor our partnership with Israel, as God said He will bless those who bless Israel and curse those who curse her (Gen. 12:3).

SWEET FREEDOM IN *Action*

Today, thank God for the blessing of friendship. Pray for the protection of our friend Israel, and show your support for her.

The Value of Hard Work

For even when we were with you, we gave you this rule: "The
one who is unwilling to work shall not eat."
2 Thessalonians 3:10

One of the first descriptions of God in Genesis is that He's a worker. ("By the seventh day God had finished the work he had been doing; so on the seventh day he rested from all his work.") Jesus was also a laborer, a carpenter...and at times, a commercial fisherman! He worked hard to put food on the table.

God commands, and commends, hard work. Today, many Americans are hitting the pavement looking for work. But some unashamedly think that they're owed a living and rely on a bankrupt government and hard-pressed taxpayers to support them. How long do you think that can last?

That didn't fly then in Thessalonica, and it shouldn't fly today. When government enables people who *can* work *not* to work, what it's really doing is undermining the moral character of our country. God expects us to take care of ourselves, to have a work ethic, and of course to help those truly in need—but not to subsidize lazy, selfish, immoral lifestyles.

Let's just admit God knows better than we do, and we can do it His way and save a lot of grief.

Give thanks that you have a job. And if you're looking for a job, remember that for every one of us, there's a job out there. It might not be the one we want, but it could be the one we need.

Today, model a good work ethic for your kids. Don't let them lie around the house doing nothing. Teach the value of working, saving, and giving. Even the youngest children can learn!

DOING MY PART

*But so that we may not cause offense, go to the lake and
throw out your line. Take the first fish you catch; open its
mouth and you will find a four-drachma coin. Take it and give
it to them for my tax and yours.*

Matthew 17:27

"We commercial fish," Todd is known to say. "There's no time for
sport because we don't play with our food."

I love to fish and believe a bad day fishing beats a good day...well,
doing most anything else. But commercial fishing is hard, cold, exhausting
work...and Jesus knew it, too.

That's why I find this story so interesting.

Jesus told Peter to go fish and said he'd find a coin in the first fish's
mouth. I would love to have seen Peter's reaction. But surely, if Jesus could
make a fish cough up a coin, He could have simply made the money appear
out of thin air.

Instead, He utilized Peter's skill.

We can't just sit back and expect God—or government, no matter how
well meaning—to place everything in our hands. God expects us to take
action. He doesn't drive parked cars.

As we do what we can, He does what we can't, often moving miracu-
lously. It's beyond awesome to see God work in this way!

As the saying goes, "God helps those who help themselves."

SWEET FREEDOM IN *Action*

Today, make a charitable donation to a group that helps people, dis-
abled or able-bodied, find the dignity of work.

MY JOB SUCKS (PARAPHRASED, OF COURSE)
Commit to the Lord whatever you do,
and he will establish your plans.
Proverbs 16:3

As honoring as work is, sometimes every day feels like Monday. I get it. I've made five cents a flat picking strawberries in mosquito-infested mud; I've janitored tobacco-tinged office buildings; I've set nets, slayed salmon, and gritted my teeth and refused to tell my captain—in fisherman's language, no less—how I *really* feel when covered in slimy scales in Bristol Bay. At work, each new day brings with it a choice.

God plants us in uncomfortable places for His purpose. Maybe you can't change your circumstances today, but you can change your attitude. Be a light unto others! Do your coworkers need to see real hope? Do they know Jesus? Fill yourself with God's Word. Study Joshua. Talk to God as you would your closest friend. Ask Him to have His way in your workplace. Though your situation seems gloomy, God is working it all out for your good, and for the good of those around you. Shake off the slime and trust God where you work.

SWEET FREEDOM IN *Action*

Today, pray that God intervenes in your workplace to provide hope, inspiration, and understanding for those laboring alongside you.

SHEPHERDLESS SHEEP

When Jesus landed and saw a large crowd, he had compassion
on them, because they were like sheep without a shepherd.
So he began teaching them many things.

Mark 6:34

A father looks at his children and, seeing a need, does everything to meet it, not unlike a shepherd. To understand fully Jesus's reaction to the multitude, understand the nature of sheep: These stubborn animals are slow to learn, copycats, dependent.... I think they're even whiny. Not exactly the stuff of impressive résumés. No wonder Jesus was filled with compassion.

Our culture is not unlike what Jesus saw in His: masses of people who arrogantly chart their own course. They often pursue whatever the current trend is, with no moral compass. No matter how many times their methods, ideas, or policies fail, they refuse to about-face. Remember, sheep are dense and stubborn. Perhaps it's their dependency that moved Jesus most. Sheep cannot live without a shepherd. We all know that without our Shepherd, the Lord, we would be lost. Jesus knows our predicament, and He is filled with compassion for us. He knows that we need teachers and preachers; and He knows that because we're sheep, we're stubborn and slow to learn. But He will never give up on us if we don't give up on Him.

SWEET FREEDOM IN *Action*

Today, submit to the Shepherd's leadership. He uses His rod and staff to correct and prod, but our obedience is rewarded with grace and joy and life everlasting.

HMMM, DR. SPOCK OR JESUS . . . ?

*But as for you, continue in what you have learned and have
become convinced of, because you know those from whom
you learned it, and how from infancy you have known
the Holy Scriptures, which are able to make you wise for
salvation through faith in Christ Jesus.*
2 Timothy 3:14–15

The best day of my life was April 20, 1989. That was the day I became a mom. I haven't had a solid night's sleep since. Becoming a parent gave me much more sympathy for what we kids put Mom and Dad through over the years. Maybe that's why Dad has a sign in his entryway: *I Child-proof My Home, But They Keep Finding A Way In.*

We worry about our kids: Are we too strict? Not strict enough? We watch them go from depending on us for everything to a time when they don't seem to need—or want—us at all. Sometimes it's hard letting go and trusting God with them. We need not fear, though; we place them in the ultimate capable hands. As much as we love them, God loves them even more. So we release them to Him and believe that what we have imparted in them remains.

SWEET FREEDOM IN *Action*

Today, take a break from reading the "how to parent" books and double down on your time with God. His Holy Spirit will guide you through this precious, over-too-quickly chapter of life. And the pages do turn, so be patient through those arduous, exhausting days—and nights—of early motherhood, especially. When you get to be my age, you'll see—the days were long but the years flew by.

Wanted: Shield against College Debt and Indoctrination

No one can serve two masters. Either you will hate the one
and love the other, or you will be devoted to the one and
despise the other. You cannot serve both God and money.
Matthew 6:24

It took me five years to graduate college, because I worked throughout to pay for it. All my siblings did; there was never a question about Dad's teacher salary covering four kids in college at once. We did the math...we all got jobs. Nowadays, parents unload boatloads of money on a kid's "college experience," and that "experience" has never been costlier.

Not just financially. Modern college culture often involves nonstop efforts to unravel our children's value systems. Self-indulgence is the name of the game, with professors blatantly attempting to indoctrinate with their liberalism. College today isn't necessarily an incredibly rigorous experience, where students' minds are constantly challenged and their horizons broadened. So many courses are so politically correct they don't even pass the straight-face test. Since really buckling down to take silly courses isn't required, much time is dedicated to just having a good time— to partying. Many professors have cushy jobs that don't require them to, you know, actually *teach*. That means parents spend their hard-earned money—or, more accurately, borrow their *not-yet-earned* money—for grad students and adjuncts to fill the role of educator. You getting what you paid for, Pops?

And for all of this, the student-loan debt in America is nearly $1 trillion! It's prudent to think twice before shelling out big bucks to liberals so they can enjoy efforts to brainwash the next generation.

Today, teach kids the value of higher education, making sure they value God's Truth over the falsehoods of man. Consider creative ways to pay for education—such as, ummm, getting a job. It teaches them the value of what they're receiving, and even possibly keeps them from blowing cash when the keg party passes the hat.

MAMA GRIZZLY: HEAR HER ROAR

*Start children off on the way they should go, and even when
they are old they will not turn from it.*
Proverbs 22:6

A s governor, I stood on the grassy bank of a pristine waterway teeming
with salmon, taking notes with Department of Fish and Game personnel. Right in front of us were forty-two bears foraging, fighting, feeding,
and fending off enemies to survive. Even a lifelong Alaskan gets excited
about that! The "mama bears" are the hardest workers on the water.

Mama grizzlies don't wait for another bear to do the work for them,
they fend for themselves and their cubs, preparing for winter. Sows instinctively rear up on hind legs when cubs are threatened. And most important,
they teach their young how to fish for a lifetime. It's fascinating watching
them. The males, too, but they're usually occupied comparing the size of
their catch and hanging out downriver in man caves, or, I mean, bear caves.

We could all learn a lot from mama grizzlies who teach their young to
provide for themselves, protect themselves, and save up for lean times.

SWEET FREEDOM IN *Action*

Today, teach your children—or a child in need who might not have a
responsible parent or mentor—the virtue of self-sufficiency.

BROKEN HEARTS FIXED HERE
He heals the brokenhearted and binds up their wounds.
Psalm 147:3

God's healing is not limited to the physical. He makes us whole—body, soul, and spirit. He needs us delivered from the pain of our past so we may live vibrantly and minister out of a pure and enthusiastic heart. To be healed, hand it to Him: past broken hearts, public failures, stalled dreams, regretful steps backward. I doubt I'm alone with some of my memories having been so painful that it physically hurt to let them brush across my heart and mind again. When it does still ache like that, more complete healing is here.

I have a gnarly thrashed ankle that's an old badge of honor from a hard-fought high school basketball victory about a hundred years ago. I can hobble along on it just fine, even insisting on navigating icy parking lots in four-inch heels, and no one can tell there was ever a problem. But some days, something twists and I wail. Why?

Because there's still a problem: my ankle was never allowed to fully heal. Our spiritual and emotional selves can be like this. We seem fine, until somebody twists something, perhaps callously saying or even innocently doing something that triggers the pain of the past. Those old insecurities, abuses, regrets—they rise and we lash out. Jesus sets us free so we don't have to spend a lifetime appearing whole outwardly while our hearts remain broken.

SWEET FREEDOM IN *Action*

Today when that twinge of hurt catches your breath, don't just stop there. Take your breath *deep* and tell God you acknowledge the brokenness and you're ready now for complete healing.

DISCIPLES RIDING SHOTGUN

*Simon Peter, Thomas (also known as Didymus), Nathanael
from Cana in Galilee, the sons of Zebedee, and two other
disciples were together. "I'm going out to fish," Simon Peter
told them, and they said, "We'll go with you." So they went
out and got into the boat, but that night they caught nothing.*
John 21:2–3

Halibut fishing in Cook Inlet is about the most fun a law-abiding American can have. It takes a few of us working together to haul the gaffed heavy white meat up and over the boat rail and club it before the fish slaps us overboard. Then, tradition dictates, your crew sits around a bonfire eating s'mores, watching one pro (wouldn't be me) start filleting. The beauty of catching our own is there's always plenty of that fresh organic food for everyone. We just have to club it first.

It doesn't take a village to catch a fish, but it's fun to have one to eat it up. That's why I love the Scripture passage above. When Peter said he was going fishing, his friends said, "Wait up! We're coming too!" Someone called shotgun and they were off.

In fishing—like life—it helps to have loved ones around…to process the bounty or survive disappointment when you get skunked.

SWEET FREEDOM IN *Action*

Today, when someone asks for help, and someone will, join in. Be a good friend who helps in times of need and celebrates in times of joy. It takes reaching out. God gives those opportunities to love your friends and family well.

COURAGE IS A VIRTUE

*Have I not commanded you? Be strong and courageous. Do
not be afraid; do not be discouraged, for the Lord your God
will be with you wherever you go.*

Joshua 1:9

When I think of courage, I often think of the Greatest Generation—a generation that lived through a Great Depression, that endured the shock of the attack at Pearl Harbor, and that took up the challenge thrown down by Japan, Nazi Germany, and fascist Italy, and fought a giant world war to defend our freedom and liberty and that of our allies.

And of course for many American servicemen, it didn't end there. Not long after World War II, Communist North Koreans invaded South Korea, and many veterans of the Second World War were in uniform again, fighting for another country's freedom.

Too many of us forget their sacrifices and the sacrifices of our men and women who continue to serve in uniform and die on foreign battlefields. Not only should we remember their sacrifices, we should emulate their courage.

I believe these men instinctively knew the principle about which Joel Osteen later wrote: "No matter how many times you get knocked down, keep getting back up. God sees your resolve. He sees your determination. And when you do everything you can do, that's when God will step in and do what you can't do."

SWEET FREEDOM IN *Action*

Today, call on God to give you strength and courage for the day ahead—and give thanks for all those who have served, and who continue to serve, our country.

LETTING NONBELIEVERS NOT BELIEVE

*And he sent messengers on ahead, who went into a
Samaritan village to get things ready for him; but the people
there did not welcome him, because he was heading for
Jerusalem. When the disciples James and John saw this, they
asked, "Lord, do you want us to call fire down from heaven
to destroy them?"*

Luke 9:52–54

Jesus "turned around and rebuked" James and John when they wanted to call down fire from heaven to destroy an unwelcoming Samaritan village.

That's not the way you make converts. You do it by living the Christian life with joy. It's by our words, deeds, and example that we show what faith in Christ is all about.

America is all about sweet freedom, and so is God.

God wants us to choose Him of our own free will. Respect that. If God won't force us to have faith, neither should we think that we can, or should, force anyone else.

SWEET FREEDOM IN *Action*

Today, rejoice in the freedom God has given us, and ask Him that you and I and all Christians might set an example that will encourage others to heed God's call.

TAKE UP ARMS, SO SAYS JESUS

He said to them, "But now if you have a purse,
take it, and also a bag; and if you don't have a sword,
sell your cloak and buy one."
Luke 22:36

I encourage people to carry a gun...because a cop is too heavy.

Jesus told His disciples to be ready to defend themselves. He wanted them armed in case they had to beat back thieves, cutthroats, and other bad guys. They didn't hide their swords; they were, you might say, practitioners of open carry!

Jesus wasn't delicate, vulnerable, or timid. My husband, Todd, often points out that all those much later artistic depictions of Jesus with long shiny hair, flowing robes, and flip-flops give exactly the wrong impression. Jesus is Lord. He is King. He is a warrior and our protector. He is God Almighty. He is our fortress, our refuge, our strength. He withstood the devil. He triumphed over death. His Word is victory.

SWEET FREEDOM IN *Action*

Today, remember that God always wants what is best for us—and that includes our safety. We should follow the example of His disciples and be ready to defend ourselves and our loved ones from evil.

The Old Testament and the Second Amendment

If a thief is caught breaking in at night and is struck
a fatal blow, the defender is not guilty of bloodshed.
Exodus 22:2

You might have seen the bumper sticker that says, "When seconds count, police are only minutes away." That statement is a simple truth, especially in rural America. Solely relying on others to protect you is an astoundingly unsafe, naïve practice.

Liberals often act as though it's sinful to arm oneself for protection, which is why, despite our Second Amendment right to keep and bear arms, they push relentlessly for ever more restrictions on gun ownership.

We've seen that Jesus ordered His disciples to arm themselves with swords. In the Old Testament, the justice of self-defense is taken for granted. Most Americans know this in their hearts, in their bones; they know that self-defense is a natural right. Don't let confused liberals tell you otherwise.

God wants us to be protectors of the weak and innocent. To do that effectively you need to be ready; you need to be armed; and you need to know how to use a weapon to defend yourself and your loved ones.

Sweet Freedom in *Action*

Today, commit to supporting organizations and leaders who fight for our Second Amendment and oppose those who seek to destroy it.

ISLAMIC JIHADISM IS EVIL INCARNATE

*...what kinds of things happened to me in Antioch, Iconium
and Lystra, the persecutions I endured. Yet the Lord rescued
me from all of them. In fact, everyone who wants to live a
godly life in Christ Jesus will be persecuted....*
2 Timothy 3:11–12

Who'd rather read, "The godly shall *never* suffer persecution"? Me. But we do. So did Christians in the time of the apostles. And they are suffering now—around the world, but especially under the lash of Islamic terrorism.

Who, just a few years ago, could have imagined the so-called Islamic State—or ISIS, or ISIL, or Daesh, or whatever you want to call it—appearing on the scene and literally crucifying Christians, including children; or that they would brag about beheadings; or that they would be committing mass executions of Christians? That's evil incarnate—but the big-dog media don't like to talk about it, and neither do liberal politicians.

And that's only one strand of Islamic terrorism. There's al Qaeda and there are other jihadist movements, all of which are dedicated to the extermination or subjugation of Christians. There's a global war against Christianity in the name of Islam—and a lot of us don't even know about it, because the lamestream media don't think it's newsworthy.

SWEET FREEDOM IN *Action*

Today, challenge yourself to keep informed about the Jihadist threat. Pray for courage, pray for God's protection of our country, pray for our leaders to defeat this death cult, and pray for threatened Christians around the world.

Public Schools—Arenas of Hope

The student is not above the teacher, but everyone who is
fully trained will be like their teacher.
Luke 6:40

I come from a family full of teachers. Both my parents were involved in education—Dad as a science teacher and coach—and I also had grandparents and siblings who went into that noble profession as well.

I know. Good teachers make all the difference.

We've been blessed to have great educators in Alaska—including our local high school history teacher who inspired my son with his dramatic retelling of American history and emphasis on American exceptionalism. That played a big part in my son's decision to enlist in the military. He is now a combat veteran and sees his career path in defending America's security.

We need good teachers all across this country! They are the ones who, along with parents, are the most instrumental in informing the next generation. Will that generation understand and respect our Constitution? Will they have been taught honest, accurate history that illustrates just how exceptional a country America has been? Or will they be indoctrinated into thinking that the United States is no better than any other nation, maybe even worse, and in need of a transformation at the hands of liberal big government?

Sweet Freedom in *Action*

Today, vow to get involved with your local school board, pray for our hardworking teachers, get to know good teachers in your community, and do something special for them!

SHOULD I BE THANKFUL? HMM, LET ME THINK.

*Finally, brothers and sisters, whatever is true, whatever
is noble, whatever is right, whatever is pure, whatever is
lovely, whatever is admirable—if anything is excellent or
praiseworthy—think about such things.*
Philippians 4:8

Terrorist attacks, a failing economy, illegal immigration, government overreach—people say it's hard to find anything praiseworthy to think on today. God, however, has given us an abundance of praiseworthy things to consider, and don't you think it offends Him when we think otherwise? Let's open our eyes! We're still the most privileged nation in the world. We still have freedom to praise His name and preach the truth in love. He has blessed us with a nation that was founded on *His* principles.

SWEET FREEDOM IN *Action*

Here's a healthy exercise: Today, make a list of things for which you are grateful... or maybe things for which you *should* be grateful. Think about each item, thank God for each, and train your brain to meditate on gratitude. Ahhhh, what a better day you will have.

SARAH, QUIT TALKING

...if my people, who are called by my name, will humble
themselves and pray and seek my face and turn from their
wicked ways, then I will hear from heaven, and I will
forgive their sin and will heal their land.

2 Chronicles 7:14

I *love* this promise from God! It brings such hope to a hurting nation. All God asks us to do is humble ourselves, acknowledge we need Him, pray, and turn from our wicked ways—and He *will* restore our land! We all have a part to play in making this happen, to turn our nation back to the very One upon whom it was founded. It's been said, "Preach the Gospel, and if you have to—use words," meaning we must be stronger salt and brighter light out there in the world *by our actions*. No more just preaching to the choir. Get out of your comfort zone and connect with a lost and dying people. Many are confused and simply looking for what is *real*, for *Truth*, for the only thing that can bring salvation. Show them a real relationship with God. *Showing* them is key. The old saying is true: actions speak louder than words.

SWEET FREEDOM IN  *Action*

Today, let's not just *try* but let's *succeed* in ending our arrogant ways that turn others away from God. Turn down the volume; don't let our words get in the way of His real message.

GOD DOESN'T WEAR YOGA PANTS
She sets about her work vigorously;
her arms are strong for her tasks.
Proverbs 31:17

We're expected to exercise for the strength—spiritual, mental, physical—to tackle God-given tasks. In *no* area are we productive when we're lazy. But society often gets it backward—obsessed with the physical, while ignoring the soul. God puts a premium on the latter.

"Charm is deceptive, beauty is fleeting," we've heard. Or, as Mom says, "Beauty is only skin-deep."

The Bible says a woman who fears (meaning "is in awe of") the Lord is beautiful and shall be strong and firm. I sometimes get caught up in an obsession with exercise, especially running and isometrics in a hot, hot Bikram room. I've justified time spent doing it by acknowledging it lets me think, and formulate productive plans, and pray. This is all good and true.

But when I feel anxious, impatient, and totally on edge if I'm unable to run, it's not good. It means I've taken it too far.

I so often say, "Sweat is my sanity!" But could that mean I'm letting workouts take the place that should be filled by God?

We need balance between body, mind, and soul—and of those three, the soul is by far the most important. No other thing, even a good thing like exercise, should come before our relationship with God. God is found in prayer, not in neon lace-ups and stretchy pants.

SWEET FREEDOM IN *Action*

Today, pledge to spend at least as much time in prayer as you do at the gym.

OH, CRY ME A RIVER

*Bear with each other and forgive one another if any of you has
a grievance against someone. Forgive as the Lord forgave you.*
Colossians 3:13

So I wasn't overly sympathetic. Can you blame me?

I was talking to a young lady who was devastated after a Facebook comment dissed her appearance.

"Umm, they didn't like your new 'do'?" I feigned understanding. "How many Facebook followers you got there?"

"Three," she said.

OhDearLordJesusSpareMe.

Big hurts and little hurts, we've all got 'em.

I won't bore you with my own bumps and bruises, but a wealth of "Palin stuff," true or not, paraded before the world, seemingly on a regular basis, gives me experience to help others persevere.

God can use indignities for His purposes! One way to survive is to keep your perspective. Kissing a firstborn goodbye—off to war; cradling a newborn struggling with special needs; preparing for a teenager's pending motherhood; governing the nation's largest state; and campaigning for vice president of those states...all at once, Lord? This, while ruthless rumormongers felt big by making others feel small.

How to handle all that?

My "sufferings" are minuscule compared to others: those who have lost a family member in military service, or lost a child, or who are single moms with no supportive family to help them.

It's hard for all of us to keep perspective. But one way to gain perspective is to get out there and help other people.

Today, volunteer for people who are *really* hurting, hurting worse than you are. Don't dwell on anything out of your control—especially don't worry about what people say about you. Give it all to God. And, darling Piper, ignore Facebook slights about your purple hair.

UNITY IN COMMUNITY

I urge you to live a life worthy of the calling you have received. Be completely humble and gentle; be patient, bearing with one another in love. Make every effort to keep the unity of the Spirit through the bond of peace.
Ephesians 4:1–3

Alexis de Tocqueville believed the strength of American democracy rested in the tendency of its citizens from all walks of life to pursue unity. He observed that when Americans had an idea, their first step was to unite, knowing isolated individuals are far more vulnerable to failure than those who are unified in purpose. Tocqueville goes so far as to say that civilized society depends on the "art of association."

We might use different words, but we all know this is true. We see it at a small-town BBQ when neighbors gather to talk about the issues they face. We see it when a town gets behind its underdog football team and cheers it to victory.

God says His people are blessed when they walk together in unity (Ps. 133:1). Don't you yearn for that? Let's strive to walk unified with other believers, knowing we are stronger together than alone.

SWEET FREEDOM IN *Action*

Today, work through and get over petty differences with your neighbor. Walk worthy of your calling by engaging with friends, family, and community, in unity.

Pilgrim's Progress beyond Comfort Zones

*... they only saw them and welcomed them from a distance,
admitting that they were foreigners and strangers on earth.
People who say such things show that they are looking for
a country of their own. If they had been thinking of the
country they had left, they would have had opportunity to
return. Instead, they were longing for a better country—a
heavenly one. Therefore God is not ashamed to be called
their God, for he has prepared a city for them.*
Hebrews 11:13–16

America's early settlers, its Founders, its pioneers, all sought freedom and opportunity in a new land. Talk about leaving their comfort zones! Hopeful aspirations fueled their journeys. Recently, I crossed the Rocky Mountains and wondered about the hardy women who traveled long days over tortuous terrain, nursing babies, cooking for families, making and mending and cleaning clothes, and teaching and entertaining children, as they trekked across our country to start new lives in new farms, towns, and cities. Imagine the difficulties—especially having no juice boxes and iPads to distract the kids!

They had a hopeful vision that gave them the energy to press on. God wants to plant in your spirit a similar vision of a heavenly city. We pray for a transformed America, but there is hope beyond our republic—a city whose builder and maker is God.

SWEET FREEDOM IN *Action*

Ask God to create in you a pilgrim spirit anchored in the hope of our future heavenly city. Today, pray for our exceptional nation, while knowing there's hope beyond our republic—in the city whose builder and maker is God (Heb. 11).

BY THE SWEAT OF THEIR BROW YOU SHALL TAX THEM?
This is also why you pay taxes, for the authorities are
God's servants, who give their full time to governing.
Romans 13:6

Onerous taxes hurt hard workers, slam job creators, and make us less competitive against other nations. High government spending is unsustainable and leads to national bankruptcy. Printing more dollars only leads to inflation and squeezes out private borrowing. High taxes, excessive regulation, and an ever-expanding welfare state discourage enterprise and undermine our nation's work ethic.

Politicians and bureaucrats always want to expand the size of government, and they will take inaction on our part—our failing to protest against taxes, regulations, and unnecessary government programs—as not only a sign of approval, but a signal to expand government's reach even further.

Only when a law contradicts God's higher authority can we disobey it, and our obligation to pay taxes doesn't rise to that level, doggone it.

But what we can do is elect politicians willing to support freedom, reward hard work, and honor savings and investment by rolling back unnecessary taxes, government programs, and regulations. To do that, we need to do more than vote; we need to volunteer on campaigns, and we need to help educate our neighbors, friends, and community about the consequences we all suffer when government plays fast and loose with our tax dollars. We need to show how big government is unjust government, robbing hardworking Peters to pay bureaucrat-preferred Pauls.

SWEET FREEDOM IN *Action*

Today, consider getting involved in a campaign, and spread the word that the best and most just government is a small government.

THE SECOND AMENDMENT DETERS EVIL

Woe to those who call evil good and good evil,
who put darkness for light and light for darkness,
who put bitter for sweet and sweet for bitter.
Isaiah 5:20

In 2015, in a BBC interview, President Barack Obama said that he felt "frustrated" and "stymied" in failing to get the gun control laws he wanted. In fact, he said, "The United States of America is the one advanced nation on earth in which we do not have sufficient common-sense, gun-safety laws. Even in the face of repeated mass killings. And you know, if you look at the number of Americans killed since 9/11 by terrorism, it's less than 100. If you look at the number that have been killed by gun violence, it's in the tens of thousands."

You read that right: Barack Obama said that American gun owners are a bigger threat to our safety than are Muslim terrorists; and he said that Americans who believe in the Second Amendment lack "common sense."

My first response is that this just exposes how liberals like Obama have no grasp of the reality of the terrorist threat. They downplay the dangers of Islamist terrorism.

Second, they have no respect for the Constitution. They treat that noble document with contempt.

Third, they fail to consider how many crimes are prevented, deterred, or foiled by gun owners.

Scholar John Lott has shown repeatedly that in American cities, in his famous phrase, more guns equals less crime. That's a fact.

SWEET FREEDOM IN *Action*

Today, consider getting a carry permit for protection, and maybe take a friend to a range to enjoy some safe shooting. Self-defense is a God-given right guaranteed by the Constitution. Don't let liberals take it away.

RUSH TO SOLUTIONS

… and to make it your ambition to lead a quiet life:
You should mind your own business and work with your hands,
just as we told you, so that your daily life may win the respect of
outsiders and so that you will not be dependent on anybody.

1 Thessalonians 4:11–12

Rush Limbaugh nailed it on his broadcast: "Obamacare is not about improved healthcare or cheaper insurance or better treatment or insuring the uninsured, and it never has been about that. It's about statism. It's about expanding the government. It's about control over the population. It is about everything but healthcare."

Obamacare is just one part of the unwanted, unnecessary, unaffordable fundamental transformation of America hoisted upon us; its premise is unquestionable government control over a free people.

Limbaugh's message echoes that of early nineteenth-century minister William John Henry Boetcker: "You cannot strengthen the weak by weakening the strong…. You cannot build character and courage by taking away man's initiative and independence…. You cannot help men permanently by doing for them what they could and should do for themselves."

Good leaders understand that the ills of our economy and our society won't be solved by a bigger, more intrusive government. The answer to restoring America is to restore her values of freedom, hard work, and individual initiative.

SWEET FREEDOM IN *Action*

Today, get more informed about how big government is antithetical to America's foundational principles. Work to elect leaders who promise (and then deliver!) to rein in government, repeal Obamacare, and return power to the people, who can make better decisions for themselves, their families, and their businesses than bureaucrats ever will.

TRAGIC RACISM HERETOFORE IGNORED
Rich and poor have this in common:
The Lord is the Maker of them all.
Proverbs 22:2

Planned Parenthood's founder Margaret Sanger was a racial eugenicist, a proponent of the idea that through birth control, abortion, and sterilization of the "unfit" we could create a "cleaner" human race and enable "the cultivation of the better racial elements." She actually addressed this with the Ku Klux Klan.

Yet far from repudiating Sanger, liberal leaders defend her. Hillary Clinton expresses great admiration for her; Barack Obama praises Planned Parenthood and asks God to bless what they do; the *New York Times* has mentioned Sanger as a replacement for Andrew Jackson on the twenty-dollar bill.

When the media went into hysterics trying to ban the Confederate Battle Flag—while simultaneously ignoring the revelations about Planned Parenthood harvesting the organs of aborted babies, and babies born alive, for profit—I posted a graphic of the rebel flag alongside the Planned Parenthood logo with this question: "Which symbol killed 90,000 black babies last year?"

Our government—using your tax dollars—is not to be subsidizing abortion. It's illegal and immoral. Yet, Planned Parenthood receives more than a million tax dollars out of your pocket every single day. It shouldn't get a penny.

Good news: light now shines on this darkness. The abortionists were caught on tape nibbling lunch and sipping wine while nonchalantly pondering where to spend the profits made from bartering the bodies of innocent babies...just another day at the office. I know that it sounds unbelievable, like something from a macabre horror movie script—but the exposé must stir you to action, lest a nation, through complacency, accept the most revolting mission of Margaret Sanger.

SWEET FREEDOM IN *Action*

Today, don't just pray for unborn children. Demand that Congress stop funding abortion mills; elect a pro-life president; support pro-life centers that provide resources to give parents a *real* choice in this debate—knowing that choosing life is ultimately the beautiful choice.

The Rising Spirit of Adoption

But Ruth replied, "Don't urge me to leave you or to turn back from you. Where you go I will go, and where you stay I will stay. Your people will be my people and your God my God."

Ruth 1:16

If we want to fundamentally restore America, we need to ensure that no mother feels that the only response to an unplanned pregnancy is to end the life of her unborn child. There's a far better answer, and that is adoption and loving foster care. There are many families eager to adopt children, and churches across the country have made adoption a priority. There is no such thing as an unwanted child—we just need to make sure young mothers recognize that there are parents out there willing to help them and to adopt their son or daughter.

Someday soon, I believe, abortion will be seen the same way that we view slavery—as a moral evil that America should never have tolerated. The Left always likes to talk about conservatives being on the "wrong side of history." But a civilized society does not accept the butchering of babies, and there is no way that saving the lives of our littlest sisters and brothers in the womb can be on the "wrong side of history."

Sweet Freedom in *Action*

What can you do? You can think and pray seriously about adopting or fostering a child. You can volunteer to work with a local adoption program, or start one in your area. Every child deserves to have an adult mentor and guide. Be that person.

ABORTION KILLS MORE THAN THE BABY

For the wages of sin is death, but the gift of God is
eternal life in Christ Jesus our Lord.

Romans 6:23

Pop star Nicki Minaj told *Rolling Stone* about her abortion: "It was the hardest thing I have ever gone through.... It has haunted me all my life."

Aerosmith singer Steven Tyler talked about his girlfriend's abortion: "It's a major thing when you're growing something with a woman, but they convinced us that it would never work out and would ruin our lives.... You go to the doctor and they put the needle in her belly and they squeeze the stuff in and you watch. And it comes out dead. I was pretty devastated. In my mind, I'm going, Jesus, what have I done?"

Jesus.

Steven's onto something.

God forgives with such unfathomable mercy. Thank you, oh Lord. As more parents acknowledge pain and regret over their abortions, I remind them that God can lift that burden. Mothers and fathers wounded by abortion can accept the grace and forgiveness of our loving Father God.

SWEET FREEDOM IN *Action*

Pray for unwed mothers; encourage them, if you know them personally; and support programs that help mothers realize that there are much better alternatives to abortion, alternatives that offer life, love, and freedom from guilt.

WE THE PEOPLE PULL THE CORD
…there is no one who understands;
there is no one who seeks God.

Romans 3:11

T he Founding Fathers didn't think too highly of human nature, so they created three branches of government to keep power-hungry officials in check. They also slipped another "check" on these politicians into the Constitution.

Remember learning how the Constitution can be amended through Congress? Well, even better, there's a lesser-known way to change it when necessary, without Congress or the president stopping "We the People." Our Founders knew government could grow so drunk on its own power that it wouldn't ever voluntarily restrict itself, so constitutionalist George Mason allowed for a "Convention of States" in Article V to give the power back to the people.

My friend Mark Levin describes this: "By giving the state legislatures the ultimate say on major federal laws, on major federal regulations, on major Supreme Court decisions, should 3/5 of state legislatures act to override them within a two year period, it doesn't much matter what Washington does or doesn't do. It matters what you do…the goal is to limit the entrenchment of Washington's ruling class." Keep educating the people, Mark!

SWEET FREEDOM IN *Action*

Today, contact your state representatives and tell them to support the Convention of States. When the federal government proves to be corrupt, incompetent, and even malicious, the only thing that can save the Constitution is the Constitution itself.

HOMEGROWN GOODNESS

*Anyone who does not provide for their relatives,
and especially for their own household, has denied the faith
and is worse than an unbeliever.*

1 Timothy 5:8

I'm all in favor of "buying local." In fact, sometimes it's our only choice in Alaska, where it takes so much time and money to ship up goods. Aside from buying local, I'm also a big believer in *deciding local*. I believe that individual states, counties, cities, towns, and communities should govern their own affairs as much as they can—that's what gives us, "We the People," a voice.

When decisions are made in some faraway bureaucracy in Washington, D.C., they're made in a bubble—too distant from the people who will actually be affected. Instead of politicians deciding healthcare plans, education systems, our retirement savings, or anything else in the comfort of their urban offices, decisions should be made as close to home as possible. You, not some bureaucrat in Washington, should be free to make your own decisions regarding your healthcare, the education of your children, and yes, even what sort of light bulbs you can use. Government bureaucrats often forget that they are "public servants" rather than our masters or our nannies.

SWEET FREEDOM IN *Action*

Today, reflect on the fact that we have a God-given right and duty to look after ourselves, our businesses, our homes, and our families. Take a vow to support elected representatives who will return power to the people and their local communities. Self-governance is what our Founders envisioned for Americans and it is what God envisions for us as well.

Soaring as Eagles

*But those who hope in the Lord will renew their strength.
They will soar on wings like eagles; they will run and not
grow weary, they will walk and not be faint.*

Isaiah 40:31

In the lower forty-eight, it's not so common to watch magnificent wild eagles soar, but we're blessed up north to see them frequently—in fact, we see them nearly every day over my home. Alaska's Chilkat Bald Eagle Preserve boasts the largest concentration of bald eagles in the world.

This Bible verse paints a vivid picture comparing the lift of eagles' wings to the strength that our love of God gives us!

The verse tells us to "hope in the Lord," which means not only to have faith, but to listen prayerfully to God's Word and to act in obedience and trust. When we hope in the Lord, He renews our strength, restores our energy, and allows us rest (the Lord "grants sleep to those he loves," Ps. 127:2). Or, as my mom reminded me (in a card I taped to a door): "Before you go to bed, give God your troubles. He'll be up all night anyway."

Sweet Freedom in *Action*

Today, hope in the Lord, pray for patience and understanding, pray that you will be obedient to His commandments, and pray for the peace of mind and soul that comes from a confident faith.

Writing the End from the Beginning
"I am the Alpha and the Omega," says the Lord God,
"who is, and who was, and who is to come, the Almighty."
Revelation 1:8

A m I the only one who's occasionally caught completely off guard? Even though we've all lived long enough, perhaps thinking, "Nothing surprises me anymore," sometimes something really does.

But God's not surprised. He's genuinely prepared, and He can prepare us. He knows the end from the beginning. He isn't caught off guard by that thing that knocked you down. He knew it was coming; believe it or not, He even prepared you for it. The struggle ahead may seem overwhelming, but He won't give you what you can't handle. Don't take my word for it—turn to biblical examples for reassurance. When Joseph was sold by his brothers, he never expected to be ruler over Egypt. When David faced Goliath with just a slingshot and stones, who'd have believed he'd be the victor? Even as Jesus was hanging on the cross, could onlookers ever believe that the bruised, bleeding, dying man was changing the entire course of human history through His death and resurrection?

Victory can come cloaked as defeat.

Sweet Freedom in *Action*

Today, you might face apparently insurmountable trials. Rest assured that the outcome will be for your good whether or not that is readily apparent. God knows our life story from beginning to end and is with us every step of the way.

IT TAKES FAITH TO BE AN ATHEIST

In the beginning God created the heavens and the earth.

Genesis 1:1

Political debates are an exciting part of a campaign, if you're a politician. I've wondered if they're as exciting for viewers, because the questions seem quite predictable—even when reporters think they're throwing curveballs, as they always do at Republican candidates.

A favorite is "Do you believe in evolution?"

What on earth does that have to do with making or administering America's laws? If it's so important to ask Republicans, why not ask Democrats their theory of the universe's origin?

Of course, it's because it's a litmus test designed to make people who believe in God look silly. That's called a "gotcha" question.

My dad was a science teacher who instilled in me a love of the natural world. At the dinner table or while out hiking a trail, he always interjected interesting facts about our amazing outdoor surroundings.

Do I believe in evolution? I certainly believe in species changing incrementally over time. But reporters, of course, aren't interested in that, or in the details of evolution; they want to know if you believe in the ol' ape-into-man theory, because they think if you say no, they've exposed you as a simpleton (and they'd be wrong), and if you say yes, they think you've contradicted the Bible (and guess what, they'd be wrong again).

The truth is that some journalists aren't interested in truth; they're just interested in gotcha.

But as believers we have a duty to the truth, and we know where to find it. (I'll give you a clue: it's in something more substantial than a newspaper or the TV news.)

Today, think for yourself, and, as the Good Book says, "Work out your own salvation with fear and trembling"—and recognize that it takes more "blind faith" to be an atheist than it does to believe that creation requires a Creator.

WHO'S SERVING WHOM?
For all those who exalt themselves will be humbled,
and those who humble themselves will be exalted.
Luke 14:11

Y ou might have noticed, but a lot of politicians have a habit of exalting themselves. They get into politics because they love power, and they stay there because they love wielding it. They think they're mafia dons who can grant us, or special interests, favors. Actually, in some ways they're worse than mafia dons because at least mafia dons don't pretend that what they do is good for the people—at least I don't think they do. But a lot of politicians certainly do that—bossing you around, taxing you, regulating you, taking away your freedom, and telling you it's all for your own good.

Don't believe it.

Just because someone holds elective office, or is a government employee, doesn't mean they're any better than you are. They might think they are, but they're not. They're supposed to be serving you—not the other way around.

Remember that a true leader is a servant leader, and that ultimately our only Lord and Master is God.

SWEET FREEDOM IN *Action*

Today, receive the wisdom of humility gleaned from Jesus, and know that you are the equal, in God's eyes, of any other man or woman.

PERSECUTION COMES—LEAN IN
If the world hates you, keep in mind that it hated me first.
John 15:18

When Jesus was on earth, He was mocked, beaten, and homeless, and He eventually faced a humiliating death.

But, He didn't run from this persecution. Instead, He looked it boldly in the face, proclaiming the Gospel all the more confidently.

So what justifies our behaving any differently? Nothing. The world will treat us as it treated Christ. As Dr. Russell Moore says, living like Jesus with "convictional kindness" will result in "a doubling of one's potential criticizers. Those who don't like the gospel call to repentance will resent the conviction, and those who don't like the gospel drive to mission will resent the kindness."

Yet, we are still called to show grace, regardless.

In the face of certain persecution, we must lean in, just as Christ did, not into ourselves, or our self-help guides, or false prophets, or any substitutes—but into God. We'll be reviled (if we're doing it right), but we'll find greater love and a sweeter resting place in God than in anything this world can offer.

SWEET FREEDOM IN *Action*

Today, read Acts 7 and be encouraged by Stephen, the Church's first martyr. Pray God will embolden us like Stephen to speak His Truth no matter the cost.

SCOOT OVER; GET OUT OF THE DRIVER'S SEAT

That is why, for Christ's sake, I delight in weaknesses,
in insults, in hardships, in persecutions, in difficulties.
For when I am weak, then I am strong.
2 Corinthians 12:10

There's nothing like the feeling you get as a mama or a daddy when a child reaches out to you. Little children, by design, are dependent on you for food, protection, and love.

Guess what, Mom and Dad: We're all designed to be dependent on God. In fact, we can't get through life without Him. If you're like me, you sometimes forget this. We think we're in control, and—just like our kids—we sometimes forget the true source of our help and protection.

Only when the winds of persecution begin to blow are we reminded of our weaknesses. In the midst of spiritual battle, we have no one else to turn to but the One really in control. We come face to face with our humanity—our limitations—and we are left seeking the strength and perspective that only comes from above.

This, friends, is actually a blessing of difficulties, hardships, insults, and persecution: we're given the opportunity to truly rely on our Maker. Persecution strips us of false notions we have about our own strength, and reminds us where the real stuff can be found—in the arms of our Heavenly Father!

SWEET FREEDOM IN *Action*

Take a break in the arms of the Father, even now. Ask for Him to take control of all areas of your life where you've insisted on being in the driver's seat.

BITTER OR BETTER THROUGH PERSECUTION

See, I have refined you, though not as silver;
I have tested you in the furnace of affliction.
Isaiah 48:10

Christians in other parts of the world risk their livelihoods, their homes, even their lives for the Gospel of Christ.

We in America might someday be called to do the same.

Persecution of Christians is happening all across the globe.

Should we try to stop Christian persecution? Of course.

Should we fear it? No, because God always turns evil to good, and persecution refines the Church. Just as a kiln burns away impurities, the fire of persecution can burn away the impurities in our own hearts. Eventually, only God's Truth remains.

Most of us know firsthand what happens to our faith when we withstand trials. My family and supporters have been mocked all over the media for standing firm to God's Truth. Yet each time we stand firm, our faith has been made stronger.

We become more humble because persecution doesn't allow room for pride. We learn God's Word better because in the midst of our storms we looked to it to set our compass. We become more loving because each time God shows up we're reminded how much He loves us.

Evangelist Beth Moore says it this way: "Only you can decide how your fires will affect you. Will you be sanctified or scarred?"

God can work all things for His good—even the persecution of His people.

SWEET FREEDOM IN *Action*

Today, donate to a charity that supports persecuted Christians; and if you are facing personal trials, seek God's purpose in them and pray that your own faith might be refined.

OVERLOOK INSULT—HOW PERSECUTION UNIFIES
Will you not revive us again, that your people may rejoice in you?
Psalm 85:6

M any people assume, using worldly logic, that the Church will shrink the more it is persecuted. But the world's logic isn't God's.

Though many have tried to destroy the Church, the Church always survives, and even, historically, has grown in the face of trouble. The example of faithful Christians is the best evangelist; unity can be forged through the fires of harassment. Pope Francis put it this way: "Today the blood of Jesus, poured out by many Christian martyrs in various parts of the world, calls us and compels us towards the goal of unity. For persecutors, we Christians are all one!"

It's easy to let insignificant details divide the Body of Christ. But when we truly face opposition from the enemy of our souls, there's no time for trivialities!

SWEET FREEDOM IN *Action*

Today, choose unity with your brothers and sisters. (Yes, even the grumpy church marm who insults your potato salad at every potluck.) Decide not to focus on irrelevant details, but instead will to stand as one with the Body of Christ, the Rock of our Salvation!

FACES OF MODERN DAY PERSECUTION

*Therefore, brothers and sisters, in all our distress
and persecution we were encouraged about you because of
your faith. For now we really live, since you are standing
firm in the Lord.*
1 Thessalonians 3:7–8

When we think of persecution, many great biblical characters come to mind: Stephen, Daniel, Shadrach, Meshach, and Abednego. Sadly, persecution didn't end with the early Church. Christians all over the world are suffering for our faith today.

Some of you might have heard of Naghmeh Abedini, a courageous American wife and mother who has campaigned for the release of her husband, Pastor Saeed Abedini, an American citizen, who has been held, beaten, and tortured in Iranian prisons simply for sharing his Christian faith.

Others might have heard of Mariam Ibraheem, who was imprisoned in horrific conditions in the Sudan and was under sentence of death for refusing to renounce her faith in Christ. She was forced to give birth to her second child while her legs were chained to the floor of her jail cell. Now she is a spokeswoman for other persecuted Christians. I have had the privilege of meeting her, and she is a woman of unbelievable grace and dignity.

Pastor Saeed's and Mariam's sufferings are but two examples of what our brothers and sisters go through in countries that are not free.

SWEET FREEDOM IN *Action*

Today, write your congressman and demand that he make the defense of religious freedom at home and abroad a priority.

LOCKED AND LOADED FOR BATTLE

But since they have no root, they last only a short time.
When trouble or persecution comes because of the word,
they quickly fall away.

Matthew 13:21

The Bible promises trials for followers of Christ, so we're wise to prepare for battle now. A soldier doesn't begin his training after he's called into battle; he's been sacrificing and preparing for months and years before his boots hit the battlefield. So, how do we put on our armor for a spiritual battle? By studying and memorizing God's Word. It forms a protective shield over our souls, warding off enemy attacks.

Many times this past year, I've had to cling to the Bible. From sad incidences like pit bulls killing our favorite family dog; to therapies not quite working to allow my youngest son to eat solid foods; to my oldest heading to Iraq again; to dangerous stalkers disrupting our lives; to parents' health issues; to getting canned from one job and not knowing what was next; to a daughter's long-awaited happy wedding that didn't happen; to biopsy results positive for cancer; to all the messed-up political and national security issues I cover in my work; to…well, a whole lot more. It's been a heck of a year, and I couldn't get through it without God's promises for a brighter day.

SWEET FREEDOM IN *Action*

Memorizing Scripture is a tool to get us through to the other side. Write verses on Post-It Notes and stick them on mirrors, the fridge, the TV. Commit to memorizing new Scripture every month so that when trials come your way, you'll be locked and loaded and ready for spiritual battle!

THAT ONE THING

"Martha, Martha," the Lord answered, "you are worried
and upset about many things, but few things are needed—
or indeed only one. Mary has chosen what is better,
and it will not be taken away from her."
Luke 10:41–42

Beep. Buzz. Ding. Ring.

The tools designed to make our lives easier distract us more and more. The past's snail mail letter arriving in the box might've sat there for a while, but now it's an e-mail, text, or tweet we're expected to respond to immediately. We're online 24/7 with alerts coming throughout the night.

When Piper was younger, she'd give me "the eye" as I focused on incoming texts and e-mails. That look meant, "Mom, you're here but you're not here." Now that she has her own phone, I often say, "Hey, Pipe, you're here but you're not here—I'm talking to you!" With the world at our fingertips, it's easy to miss those who are right before us in the same room.

In the story of Mary and Martha, one sister was in tune with what was happening while the other was caught up in busyness.

Focus on Jesus. Don't miss Him: He's here in the room with you.

SWEET FREEDOM IN *Action*

Go offline for a day—no e-mail, texts, TV, or social media. It might be an unsettling withdrawal! Ask God to help you reprioritize life and dial down so as not to miss Jesus. He's here.

HE LIKES YOU, HE REALLY LIKES YOU

*For the Lord's portion is his people, Jacob his allotted
inheritance. In a desert land he found him, in a barren and
howling waste. He shielded him and cared for him;
he guarded him as the apple of his eye.*
Deuteronomy 32:9–10

My mom found salvation in the Jesus Movement of the 1970s. In those days, it wasn't fire and brimstone scaring the hell out of folks, but the love of God drawing them into a great big community of grace. As part of an active Irish Catholic family, we'd all been baptized Catholic. Mom started watching Billy Graham crusades, and she loved the combined message of tradition and personal relationship with Christ; her passion for the faith led us all into something new. The message she received? God's crazy about you and can heal your hurts. Mom and millions of others turned to Jesus because they heard God not only loves them, but He really, really likes them! She still glows when she talks about Him.

The God who likes us never sleeps. He keeps loving watch over us every moment of every day because we are the delight of His heart. We didn't earn it—I don't deserve it—but He's always had it for us, even before we knew Him.

The prophet Zephaniah says God sings and dances over you with great joy (Zeph. 3:17)! God's emotions for His friends are expressed in the Song of Solomon—such confirming chapters to read.

SWEET FREEDOM IN *Action*

Open that Old Testament book Zephaniah today, and let the new message refresh you. It says your life brings Him great joy every day!

ETERNITY BEGINS NOW
Set your minds on things above, not on earthly things.
Colossians 3:2

S ince the fifth grade, glasses have been, and forever will be, a part of my life. I was blind as a bat before LASIK surgery years ago—it helped a bit—but the older my eyes get, the more I accept that just as I was called "four eyes" yesterday, I'll be "four eyes" tomorrow. I find now that the right lenses are needed for each different environment. Reading close up? That's one prescription. Driving at night? A different one. Distance to see a crowd or read a teleprompter? Still another. And I need tinted lenses for bright, sunny, snowy days. I'm up to trifocals now, and I doubt they make them any more newfangled than that, so my eyes had better quit aging.

Successful Christian living requires lens adjustments too—toward the eternal. An earthly perspective limits productivity because it keeps us trapped at ground level. God's view allows us to soar. An eternal perspective uses a wide-angle lens to see the big picture of what He's planned and the rewards He stores up for the faithful. Too often we're nearsighted, focusing only on the short years we have on earth, and think nothing of the years in eternity.

Theologian Art Katz said, "When we begin to see all our moments set in the context of eternity, we will bring to those moments a seriousness that we would not otherwise have had." It's time for a lens adjustment allowing us to live in the light of eternity.

SWEET FREEDOM IN *Action*

Set aside some time to evaluate your life vision, adjusting your perspective to eternity where needed.

KEEPING GOD'S WORD IN YOUR LIFE EVERY DAY
*All Scripture is God-breathed and is useful for teaching,
rebuking, correcting and training in righteousness, so that
the servant of God may be thoroughly equipped for
every good work.*
2 Timothy 3:16–17

In 2009 I handed my state's gubernatorial reins to the lieutenant governor, and it was the right thing to do. Instead of worrying about "what's next?" I had Jeremiah 29:11 to hang on to: God has a plan for our lives; it's under control; He's got this. Those years of memorizing Bible verses in Sunday school pay off in the long run! The Word of God is the foundation we all need to get life's priorities straight. I'm thankful that through all our ups and downs, the Word of God is able to direct, correct, and encourage. Like the psalmist says, "If your law had not been my delight, I would have perished in my affliction" (Ps. 119:92).

When trying to focus on God, the Bible is the best tool. Ideally, you should always have one handy: at home, in the car, wherever you are. "All Scripture is God-breathed."

SWEET FREEDOM IN  *Action*

Today, try "pray-reading" the Bible. It helps His Word come alive and invigorate our prayer life. Take a verse, read it out loud, and then turn it into a personal prayer. Speaking it out loud helps with memorizing, which keeps the Word anchored in our hearts. If you're brave, turn it into a song and sing the verses too. That's a surefire way to get it stuck in your mind.

EYES STRAIGHT AHEAD

… one thing I do: Forgetting what is behind and straining
toward what is ahead, I press on toward the goal to win the
prize for which God has called me heavenward in Christ Jesus.
Philippians 3:13–14

My dad ran a very fast Boston Marathon in the early 1980s, claiming it was extra exhilarating to have trained for it all winter amid some cruel outdoor conditions in Alaska. It toughened an already tough guy and made him appreciate the extra training effort it took to do well. He and I agree: not much compares with crossing the finish line perfectly exhausted, swearing you'll never run another one, but grinning anyway because you just checked off a bucket list item.

A New York University study found that runners who focus sharply on a point in the distance increase their speed and suffer less exhaustion. I know that when starting some of my runs, focusing on the finish line that is my driveway is literally the only thing I look forward to.

God issues the same advice for life—fix your eyes on the end game, run for the prize. Athletes can find it easy to get distracted by the crowds, the score, the stress, the aches and pains…and it's the same in life. Trials so easily beset our journey. But there is a prize at the end, and we find it as we forget what is behind and look to the eternal rewards of Jesus.

SWEET FREEDOM IN *Action*

Today, forget your worries of the moment. Breathe. Look to God. He wants to carry every one of your burdens and make the run more enjoyable.

TIE THE KNOT, HANG ON

What is mankind that you are mindful of them, human beings
that you care for them? You have made them a little lower
than the angels and crowned them with glory and honor.
Psalm 8:4–5

The midnight phone call, the unexpected doctor's report, the pink slip…in a moment, everything changes. Priorities shift. We grow, learn, adapt. That's part of life.

For some, another part is hearing the phrase *quality of life.* "Quality of life must be considered" gets tossed around after hearing, especially, an unwanted medical report, insinuating that if one's life doesn't measure up to some subjective worldly standard, it's time to cash it in.

How do you measure quality of life? Who gets to decide what's good enough? The truth is, every human life is created in the image of God, unique in every way. Inherently we're all rich with meaning and potential simply by being alive. God is *mindful* of man. He considers and ponders humanity because He loves us. If life is something that God concerns Himself with, we must value life for life's sake, not merely for some abstract concept of quality.

Though it may seem painful at first, try this: Think of seasons of your life that you might not have valued at the time. Press into the idea that God had you endure those seasons and wants you now to find their redeeming value.

SWEET FREEDOM IN *Action*

Today, if you are contemplating difficult times, ask God to reveal the purpose. He'll give you a deeper appreciation for life. He'll give you more patience to hold on. He'll bring to you other people who need the encouragement and lessons you gleaned from your trying seasons. It's for their good that you've held on.

THE WHOLE WORLD IN HIS HANDS
*Just as people are destined to die once, and after that
to face judgment....*
Hebrews 9:27

From the tiniest baby in the womb to the most powerful man in the world, we are all created in the image of God. It is an American founding belief and a universal, God-given truth that all men are created equal, endowed by their Creator with certain unalienable rights, including the rights to life, liberty, and the pursuit of happiness.

Sometimes, of course, these values come into conflict, but one man's pursuit of happiness must not take away another's right to life.

Back in 2005, the eyes of America were drawn to a Florida hospice center as a woman there fought for life. The nation met Terri Schiavo, and all were pulled into her story by the love of her family. The government got involved when her estranged husband disagreed about the value of Terri's life. The Hippocratic oath taken by medical care providers is one of the oldest, most sacred binding oaths, and it has never condoned the taking of life through lack of care. However, in this case, that oath was violated. A court ordered the removal of Terri's feeding tube. She was taken from this world too soon.

Death is not a decision for man, but an appointment set by God. To play God and hasten the process is to quench His spirit in the most tangible form we see—the life of a human being.

SWEET FREEDOM IN *Action*

Today, pray for and support faithful hospice care providers. Please visit someone whose life is of "questionable value," according to shallow worldly standards, and look into their eyes. See the spark God put there, and tell them they are loved.

"GIVE ME THE SONGS OF A NATION"

Sing for joy to God our strength; shout aloud to the God of Jacob! Begin the music, strike the timbrel, play the melodious harp and lyre.
Psalm 81:1–2

L et these two quotations wash over you:

"I am the art in your arthouses, the ideas in your institutions, the laws in your land, the message in your movies, the thoughts of your teachers, the values your kids value. I affect you. Do you affect me?"—Culture

And also this one, from the fifth-century BC Greek musician Damon of Athens:

Give me the songs of a nation, and it matters not who writes its laws.

I wish more of us—especially our politicians—realized that ideas have consequences in the real world. When we embrace certain ideals in our movies and songs (sex without restraint, for example, which happened during the "free love" 1970s), it affects our culture in ways that rules and regulations can't undo.

SWEET FREEDOM IN *Action*

Today, don't let movies, songs, and the arts be dominated by liberals. Instead, arm your Christian children and grandkids with a solid worldview and encourage them to enter these areas boldly and with excellence.

HIS BREATH IN THEIR LUNGS

*In his hand is the life of every creature and the breath of all
mankind.... Is not wisdom found among the aged? Does not
long life bring understanding?*
Job 12:10, 12

My girlfriends and I have decided that the older we get, the more we finally understand and agree with this concept of "snowbirding," so one of us needs to find a house big enough for all in a very hot locale. Our aging bones want to escape a couple Arctic winter months!

In a world placing such strong emphasis on youth, old age is a bit of a puzzle. We may not want to think about it, and we consequently may not have an appreciation for growing older. Media ads are plastered with beautiful models promoting products that promise a fountain of youth. Almost every television show, movie, or even news program is geared for those with most of their lives ahead of them.

Job says that God's hand is very much on the elderly because His breath is in their lungs. Wisdom resides in them as a result of experience but also because it takes time to understand the best of what God has to teach us. My parents have such wisdom and knowledge to pass down! I love and honor them more than they'll ever know. It'd be a tragedy to miss out on what they have to teach and offer our family and everyone else. Decades of experience are carried within what might appear to be frailer frames.

SWEET FREEDOM IN *Action*

Today, visit or call an elderly friend or relative. Ask about their lives, their stories, even their encounters with God! Listen as they tell you about the America they grew up in. Ask them for counsel on the challenges we face. God's breath *and* wisdom are in them!

GIVE ME YOUR HUDDLED MASSES

Is the law, therefore, opposed to the promises of God?
Absolutely not!
Galatians 3:21

Israel Zangwill's 1908 play *The Melting Pot* tells the story of a Russian Jew, David Quixano, and his escape to America. Quixano declares, "America is God's crucible, the great melting pot where all the races of Europe are melting and reforming...Germans and Frenchmen, Irishmen and Englishmen, Jews and Russians—into the crucible with you all! God is making the American."

So right!

In this country, people of vastly different backgrounds have found a home, a common identity, and a future. They came with different languages and customs, but many of those old distinctions faded into the background with the recognition that we had more in common than we had keeping us apart...mainly, hearts yearning for freedom and safety and following the rule of law. Out of many differences came unity, a unified nation—*e pluribus unum.*

There's a difference in pondering the status of illegal immigrants in our courts and their status in the court of heaven. They are, like us, created in the image of God, and obviously they are loved deeply and are valued as much as anyone else. Think about where *your family* was generations ago!

Being gracious to these immigrants doesn't mean we ignore our laws and the justice they provide for all, especially law-abiding immigrants. Many people coming to America are looking for a better life, but breaking the law as a first step on our soil is wrong, and it threatens their safety and ours. There *is* a better way.

SWEET FREEDOM IN *Action*

Today, pray for the welfare of legal immigrants to our country, pray for the just and proper enforcement of our immigration laws, and pledge to support politicians committed to enforcing those laws and stemming what has become an immigration crisis for us and for every Western nation.

PRAYER WARRIOR, I MAY NOT BE
This is the confidence we have in approaching God:
that if we ask anything according to his will, he hears us.
1 John 5:14

Here's a confession. Most of my prayers seem to go something like this: "God, it's me again. I'm sorry for not praying more often, but…" Then my mind wants to wander off. Am I alone in this?

Did I thaw out meat for dinner? I really need to write about the latest White House scandal. Oh, I'm sorry, God. Where were we? Oh yes—apologizing for not praying more. Shoot! I forgot macadamia nuts in Dad's favorite cookies! Did I use all the eggs?

Then, it's off to do whatever it is life demands at the moment. I try again later, with the same apology. It's not that I don't think about God—He is always on my mind. But when it comes to actually beginning an orderly prayer—and sticking to it—I just sorta get very, very distracted with life down here on earth.

I feel I'm the worst in that "can't pray" category. Thank God He doesn't expect us to be perfect prayer warriors—and thank God He wants us to do more than pray; He wants us to act. God doesn't drive parked cars! We have to go when He opens the door as He leads our lives.

SWEET FREEDOM IN *Action*

Today, set time aside for prayer. Let's shut off the phone and mental "to do" lists, and focus on the One who gives life, peace, and joy…and skills in concentration.

Our Trustworthy Father

Salvation is found in no one else, for there is no other name
under heaven given to mankind by which we must be saved.
Acts 4:12

Can you imagine so yearning for other people's salvation that you would sacrifice your only son for it? I think about my sons, and I cannot fathom being able to do something like this.

However, that's exactly what God did for all mankind. He sent His Son, Jesus Christ, to die for our sins so we will have eternal life with Him. In Genesis, chapter 22, Abraham was tested by God, and his faith led him to be willing to sacrifice his son in obedience to God. Thankfully God stopped him. Some say this test of Abraham was God's way of telling the world that He didn't require ritualistic sacrifice, as some religions did, but that He would take care of sin once and for all on the cross.

I'm no Abraham! I can't even comprehend the sacrifice, and I'm pretty sure my oldest is big enough to resist the idea anyway.

This story is sobering and inspirational. Do you spend enough time with God to know you can give Him the benefit of the doubt when circumstances seem confusing?

Sweet Freedom in *Action*

Today, let's press in together to get to know God and His nature. He proves He is good! He's got your best interests at heart; we need not doubt.

FAMILIES MATTER
Rejoice always....
1 Thessalonians 5:16

Whether on the campaign trail or camping trail, traveling to events, participating in television shows, or just being at home where life happens, as a family we try to do it all together. Sometimes it'd be easier to do things on our own, but being together has a certain intrinsic value. Plus it's always more adventurous.

Look at the population of American prisons: a tragic commonality in one cell after another is an inmate who grew up without that family network. They've only known a fractured family setting. When parents are irresponsible or absent, the next generation pays the price. Some insist that "it takes a village to raise a child," but it really just takes parents.

Families are a blessing from God. He gives children as a heritage, and parents are called a child's honor. Christian fathers and mothers who turn away from the responsible care of their children hurt them deeply. No government program in the world can fix the effects of broken families.

SWEET FREEDOM IN *Action*

Tonight, celebrate family. Keep it simple and stress-free and do something fun. Invite someone who could use the encouragement of family time. If you don't have family nearby, make the effort to get together with others, even if that means busting out of your shell and leaving your comfort zone. God designed us for fellowship.

PRESS MUTE TO HEAR THE GOOD NEWS

Let both grow together until the harvest. At that time
I will tell the harvesters: First collect the weeds and tie them
in bundles to be burned; then gather the wheat and bring
it into my barn.
Matthew 13:30

Wish there were a "good news" channel? I usually have news stations humming in the background to keep up with worldwide events, but that constant white noise is sometimes like a cloud descending on the home. I defined for Piper the term "pet peeve" a few years ago.

"Got it, Mom," she responded. "My 'pet peeve' then is Fox News."

Yikes. I turned the volume down after that one slapped me upside the head.

From crazy politicians pushing treaties with terrorist nations to thugs trashing neighborhood Walgreens in the name of "free speech," bad news is exhausting. Some days it would be nice just to hear about Joe Six Pack and his hardworking family and his kid who got an "A" in Algebra today.

Jesus tells of weeds thrown by the enemy into a field of good seed. Those weeds remind me of all the bad news we hear about in the media. As the time draws nearer to the return of Jesus, the Bible says the hearts of man will become increasingly hardened and they will refuse to repent of their crimes (Rev. 9:21).

Sorcery, murder, immorality, and theft will rise, while at the same time God's followers are called to stand firm in righteousness. Both the good seed and the bad seed will grow to fullness, until the final harvest of the "wheat." At the great harvest, according to the Word, the Lord will take up the weeds to burn them, while gathering the wheat unto Him.

SWEET FREEDOM IN *Action*

Today, stand strong in the midst of weeds; mute the droning on and on of constant bad news; and anticipate that this era's closing comments get very good for believers!

Prayer and Fasting

"Even now," declares the Lord, "return to me with all your heart, with fasting and weeping and mourning."
Joel 2:12

Fasting works. It shows God you're serious—that getting answers is more important than getting Arby's. In these troubling times the question for believers is, "How then shall we live?" What's our response to crisis supposed to be?

I'm convinced that many answers to our cultural challenges are right under our noses in black and white. The Bible gives the prescription for a nation in crisis.

Scripture prescribes fasting and gathering leaders in prayer. I always enjoyed leading prayer services on the lawn at City Hall when I served as mayor, then celebrating the National Day of Prayer on the steps of our state capitol while governor. It's refreshing and powerful when civic and religious leaders get together to ask for God's guidance. For years here in Wasilla, local pastors have gathered weekly to pray for our city.

We should always pray for our country, our respective states, and our local communities, especially that our political leaders might seek and find God's solutions to our problems

Sweet Freedom in *Action*

Today, make a small sacrifice for God, maybe by skipping lunch, or that extra cup of coffee, or that bar of chocolate. Instead of indulging yourself, offer up a prayer to God. And consider attending—or even organizing—a day of prayer with your local elected officials.

RESPONSIBILITY REQUIRED FOR DOMINION
In the beginning was the Word, and the Word was with God,
and the Word was God. He was with God in the beginning.
Through him all things were made; without him nothing was
made that has been made.
John 1:1–3

I've seen firsthand how devastating it is when people irresponsibly take from the earth with no regard for the future. Japanese fishing trawlers used to employ twenty-mile-long nets, pretty much raping the ocean floor, fishing for certain species then wasting valuable bycatch by tossing overboard the protein sources they'd netted but didn't want for market. Witnessing the foreign vessels' overfishing and waste made the rest of us commercial fishermen warn that those unsustainable practices would destroy our enormously beneficial fisheries. The foreign trawlers were made to stop.

God gave man dominion over the fish, the birds, the cattle, the land...over all the earth. That doesn't grant a right to "pillage and plunder" His bountiful creation. It's our responsibility to care for the earth and its creatures and resources, and manage it for maximum sustainability.

We're told we'll be judged for our treatment of the gifts He gives—whether that's money, time, talents, or the natural resources here on the third rock from the sun. So let's use them wisely.

SWEET FREEDOM IN *Action*

Today, look around your own property and community and start doing what needs to be done. Take your kids outdoors to pick up litter. Teach them that they have a responsibility to care for God's creation and all the many blessings that nature brings us.

DRILL, BABY, DRILL. STILL.
Indeed, the very hairs of your head are all numbered.
Don't be afraid; you are worth more than many sparrows.
Luke 12:7

Shoot, there's something I really miss about being Alaska's governor—making decisions about energy exploration. Assisting in responsibly exploiting abundant oil and gas resources is one of my favorite things to do. Really. I shared a speech in Texas with an energy industry group and lamented the federal government's refusal to expand drilling in land set aside for exactly that—drilling—and the government's stalling oil exploration in the Arctic National Wildlife Refuge (ANWR). Extreme environmentalists have the ears of too many congressmen and bureaucrats and blow the dangers of oil exploration and development hugely out of proportion. In my speech I paraphrased the Ann Coulter line that if a caribou died as a result of our expansion of domestic oil supplies, then that one caribou "could take one for the team."

You can imagine how well that went over with the environmental extremists.

God made man in His *own* image, valuing people above all else. Our stewardship over nature is part of God's plan. So, yes, we need to use care, prudence, and wisdom in developing our natural resources, but we also need to remember that our natural environment was made for us to use.

In drought-ridden California, the state government has not only failed to build adequate dams, because of environmentalist pressure, but it has actually given priority to diverting huge amounts of its scarce water reserves away from farmers and human use for the benefit of a five-inch fish! Where I come from, we call fish that size "bait."

SWEET FREEDOM IN *Action*

Today, bask in the knowledge that God cares and provides for you over all else. He's numbered the hairs on your head, knowing you so intimately! Take care of His natural resources—but don't be afraid to use them.

Global Warming? Or Cooling? Or What's It Called Now?

Command those who are rich in this present world not to
be arrogant nor to put their hope in wealth, which is so
uncertain, but to put their hope in God, who richly provides
us with everything for our enjoyment.
1 Timothy 6:17

The climate has been changing throughout history. Has man caused all these historical fluctuations in weather? No, of course not; but global warming alarmists want to make you feel responsible for natural cycles that have gone on for forever, and you need to know this is basically a moneymaker for some of them. In a way, global warming—or *climate change* as they now call it, to cover all their bases—is a pseudoscientific fad that comes complete with massive government grants and university research support for scientists, power and big budgets for bureaucrats, and a feel-good crusade for politicians. It's an unholy combination that has left truth and common sense behind.

With all the problems mankind *has* caused in this world, and all the deadly threats people currently face, claims that climate change is *our number one threat*, as the alarmists want you to believe, are downright ludicrous.

Moreover, the idea that government can "fix" our future weather patterns doesn't pass the straight-face test. Whatever government does in regulating power and siphoning off zillions of tax dollars for uneconomic, inefficient "green energy" projects will, according to some experts, chill our climate by less than two-hundredths of a degree Celsius over the course of a hundred years! And there is evidence, by the way, that our planet is entering a cooling trend anyway because of reduced solar flares and sunspot activity.

What the government's draconian regulations will actually achieve is not a healthier climate but scarcer and higher-cost energy, fewer jobs, a weaker economy, and a less secure America.

SWEET FREEDOM IN *Action*

Today, pray for sanity in the global warming debate, and do your part to get the real facts by going to writers dedicated to exposing the truth (like Breitbart's James Delingpole and Climate Depot's Marc Morano).

DRILL, BABY, DRILL REDUX

*And my God will meet all your needs according to the riches
of his glory in Christ Jesus.*
Philippians 4:19

E verything around you is touched by oil. Plastics are petroleum products. Foodstuffs and transportation of the foodstuffs, and everything
else, are dependent on oil, and, ridiculously, our nation is dependent on
foreign oil. Many Americans don't realize that our government, unlike
other countries' governments, prohibits the sale of our domestic oil on the
open market. That outdated export ban needs to end. Also needing to end
is the bureaucratic prohibition on drilling for our own safe, reliable energy
sources. Alaskans have been fighting for the right to drill on our state's
northern shore for decades. The vast majority see the government's refusal
to permit exploration and drilling as a nonsensical federal overreach.

Tapping a tiny portion of the Arctic National Wildlife Refuge (ANWR)—
two thousand acres out of nineteen million uninhabited, frozen acres—would
give us access to billions of barrels of oil that can be safely extracted and give
a huge boost to our economy and energy independence. Oil in the ground is
useless. Oil in the hands of American entrepreneurs and job creators means
new products, lower prices, and improved national security.

SWEET FREEDOM IN *Action*

Don't be governed by fear instead of faith. Today, write or call your
elected representatives and tell them to lift the ban on drilling in the
Arctic National Wildlife Refuge. It won't harm the wildlife—and it will
significantly help our country.

Government Invasion
Live as free people, but do not use your freedom as a cover-up for evil; live as God's slaves.
1 Peter 2:16

As citizens of a free nation, we cherish our right to privacy. Unfortunately, that precious right is forfeited when, for instance, our private phone records get handed to the National Security Agency (NSA) for no good reason. The NSA and FBI obtained masses of personal data on millions of innocent Americans. Supporters of this "intelligence" gathering say that we should not be concerned, because innocent people have "nothing to hide." But that's not the point. The point is that the government has no right to spy on you when you are minding your own business. As for the excuse that this invasion of privacy is necessary to prevent an act of terrorism, that's simply not proved to be true. If the FBI or the NSA suspects someone of wrongdoing, they can get a warrant to monitor that person's activities, but they have no right to spy on all of us. We the people are supposed to control our government; it is not meant to control us.

We have no secrets from God; but government is not God, and it has no right to snoop on innocent citizens.

Sweet Freedom in *Action*

God knows everything about us, but there is no good reason why some government bureaucrat should. Support elected officials who understand that government, unlike God's power, is meant to be limited and subservient to the people.

Drunk on Power

... for drunkards and gluttons become poor,
and drowsiness clothes them in rags.
Proverbs 23:21

When government limits itself to defending our lives and liberty, it creates the right environment for the people to thrive and prosper. Of course, expecting government to limit itself is like handing a chocoholic a Hershey bar and just hoping for the best.

We haven't been getting "the best." The government, binging on its own power, has insinuated itself into every aspect of life. Bureaucrats tell our children what they can eat in school (even if the kids refuse to eat it), they tell us how large our soft drinks can be (I can't imagine that's what the Founders had in mind), they shut down kids' "illegal" lemonade stands for not having a proper permit (!), and apparently they can even force us to bake cakes for events that some find immoral or wrong.

Too many people in government think it is their job to tell you what to do, what to think, and how to behave. Every bureaucrat operates under the assumption that he knows best how individual citizens should lead their lives. But that's not what freedom is all about.

Sweet Freedom in  *Action*

Today, if you have children or grandchildren, encourage them in the principle of self-reliance. Remember that whenever you—or they—get that feeling that "something must be done," you should resist the temptation of turning to government, and instead do it yourself. You can make a heck of a lot better decisions for your family than government ever can.

Providing for our Veterans

If anyone has material possessions and sees a brother or sister in need but has no pity on them, how can the love of God be in that person? Dear children, let us not love with words or speech but with actions and in truth.

1 John 3:17–18

Our veterans have served our country so courageously and admirably, so when it's our turn to reciprocate, do *they* get from *us* what's been promised? Too often, they don't. The U.S. Department of Veterans Affairs—the successor to the Veterans Administration—was exposed in 2014 as a bureaucratic, scandalous mess that offered veterans second-rate healthcare with indefensible wait times (wait times so long that some died waiting for treatment).

The Department of Veterans Affairs has emblazoned on its buildings a quotation from Abraham Lincoln: "To care for him who shall have borne the battle and for his widow, and his orphan." But as is so often the case with bureaucracies, the bureaucrats' primary goal seems to be serving themselves rather than serving the American people.

That's simply unacceptable. Our veterans fought for *us*; now we must fight for *them*.

Sweet Freedom in *Action*

Today, if you know a veteran, call him and thank him for his service, and then sit down and write a letter to your congressman asking him to ensure that our nation's veterans receive the support they deserve.

PLAYING OUR PART FOR PEACE

*There are six things the Lord hates, seven that are detestable
to him: haughty eyes, a lying tongue, hands that shed innocent
blood, a heart that devises wicked schemes, feet that are quick
to rush into evil, a false witness who pours out lies and a
person who stirs up conflict in the community.*
Proverbs 6:16–19

If there is any force in the world that is shedding innocent blood, devising wicked schemes, rushing into evil, and stirring up conflict, it is radical Islamic terrorism. From the terror attacks of al Qaeda, to the beheadings of ISIS, to the Islamist-inspired acts of violence within our own communities, radical Islam is a threat to peace-loving peoples around the world.

But with all the evil in the world, we must never feel powerless or afraid?

What can we as individuals do against the evil of Islamist terror? The answer is: a lot.

The best anti-terrorist force is a concerned citizenry. Be vigilant. If you see suspicious activities, report them to the FBI and local law enforcement. If you see an act of terrorism about to take place, intervene. We've already seen how brave Americans can thwart terror.

Protect yourself—physically and intellectually. I strongly believe that gun owning is a responsible and effective way to deter crime and even terror attacks. I also believe in the importance of keeping informed on radical Islam. Reporter Erick Stakelbeck and author Robert Spencer are two great sources.

Pope John Paul II was famous for encouraging Christians to be not afraid—and with our faith, we shouldn't be.

Today, pray for peace in the Middle East, and pray for the conversion of souls to Christ.

SCRIPTURE TALKS ORGANIZED LABOR

*Do not take advantage of a hired worker who is poor and
needy, whether that worker is a fellow Israelite or a foreigner
residing in one of your towns. Pay them their wages each day
before sunset, because they are poor and are counting on it.
Otherwise they may cry to the Lord against you, and you will
be guilty of sin.*
Deuteronomy 24:14–15

My grandfather was a union arbitrator, and I know that labor unions have done many good things. They were formed in the first place to make sure that workers had decent working conditions, reasonable hours, and fair pay.

But we all know, too, that many unions have become politicized and corrupt, even thuggish, taking advantage of mandatory union dues and pursuing agendas that don't necessarily represent the interests or beliefs of many of the workers they're supposed to represent.

Todd and I have had very good jobs where union membership happened to be mandatory. While my particular union reps practiced fairness between labor and management, I never liked the fact that union membership and dues were mandatory. I love my union brothers and sisters, but I'd much rather be unshackled and free, not part of a "closed shop."

I don't think workers should be forced to join a union. I don't think they should be forced to pay dues to support political positions they don't personally support. While I believe that labor unions have their place, more often than not I think workers can do better in a non-unionized environment. Unions nearly killed the American auto industry. Right-to-work states, on the other hand, where union membership is not mandatory, are states attractive to job creators who compete to hire the best workers. Being free to choose is a great thing—for workers as much as anyone.

Sweet Freedom in *Action*

Today, offer prayers for conscientious employees who feel forsaken by their unions, and support freedom in the workplace.

ACT TO EXTINGUISH SLAVE LABOR

The Lord detests differing weights, and dishonest scales
do not please him.
Proverbs 20:23

S lavery still exists in the world, and it is up to us as Christians to continue to fight against it. But we shouldn't kid ourselves. It's not only in distant countries that slavery is still practiced in the shadows (or in some places, like ISIS-controlled lands, even openly) but also in our own country, where human traffickers smuggle illegal immigrants over our borders, often with promises of an American Dream, while in fact handing them over to pimps or other criminals who subject them to forced prostitution or slave labor.

Obviously, the traffickers target some of the most vulnerable and innocent people for their schemes—especially young women. While trafficking is still a relatively minor problem in the United States compared with many other countries, it is still a terrible and terrifying one; it is growing rapidly; and it is something that we cannot allow. Every life is precious to God, and every innocent life deserves our support. Having fought a nation-changing war to end slavery, we should not tolerate it now, even in obscure alleyways.

SWEET FREEDOM IN *Action*

James 5:16 says the prayer of a righteous person is powerful and effective. Remain in fervent prayer for the deliverance of those enslaved in the dark reality of forced labor. Many churches are involved in fighting this evil. Support their efforts to do more to help these people escape from the clutches of today's modern-day slave masters.

FOR GOD AND COUNTRY: TIME FOR MORE TEA PARTIES!
Strike them with terror, Lord; let the nations know
they are only mortal.
Psalm 9:20

Ronald Reagan promised to restore America as a shining city on a hill. During the 2008 presidential campaign, Barack Obama promised to "fundamentally transform" our nation. He wanted to *fundamentally* change America—and alarm bells went off all across our nation, and patriotic folks rose up and found their voices. The great grassroots movement known as the Tea Party was born.

The Tea Partiers have taken a lot of media flack. I guess you could say I know something about that too. But for all the media hubbub, all the Tea Partiers want is for America's government to follow American law; they want a return to constitutional principles, inspired by biblical wisdom. Who can forget Benjamin Franklin's eloquent request for prayer before each session of the Constitutional Convention?

In part, it read: "I have lived, Sir, a long time, and the longer I live, the more convincing Proofs I see of this Truth, that God governs in the Affairs of Men. And if a Sparrow cannot fall to the Ground without His Notice, is it probable that an Empire can rise without His Aid?" At the conclusion of the Constitutional Convention, a lady approached Benjamin Franklin with a question. Had a monarchy been born, or a republic? "A republic," he told her, "if you can keep it."

This profound statement reflects the heart of the Tea Party.

SWEET FREEDOM IN *Action*

Our Founding Fathers knew that battles are won with reliance on God. Meditate on Scripture daily. Pray for our nation and her leaders. Defend constitutionalists when you see them besmirched. We serve a faithful God who hears and answers prayer!

OUR SCHOOLS ARE OUR FUTURE
Hold on to instruction, do not let it go; guard it well,
for it is your life.
Proverbs 4:13

In 2007, Steve Jobs stood before the Texas Public Education Reform Foundation and asked a provocative question: "What kind of person could you get to run a small business if you told them that, when they came in, they couldn't get rid of people that they thought weren't any good? Not really great ones, because if you're really smart, you go, 'I can't win.'... What is wrong with our schools in this nation is that they have become unionized in the worst possible way. This unionization and lifetime employment of K-12 teachers is off-the-charts crazy."

Jobs's statement was commonsense. Unfortunately, things haven't improved much since then. Some teachers unions are still strangling our public educational system, putting union interests ahead of the interests of students and hardworking teachers.

Dedicated teachers go without merit pay, and mediocre (and downright horrible) teachers are protected by tenure. Many years ago, Dad—a teacher—answered my question concerning the meaning of tenure with, "Good teachers don't need tenure." Good teachers and good schools are absolutely necessary for our future. We support our schools generously with our tax dollars. But the teachers union leadership, like that of so many bureaucracies, is seemingly concerned only with money, perks, and political power. The education of our children is way down on their list of priorities. We need to support good teachers and high educational standards, and free our schools from the tyranny of low-expectations administrators and bureaucrats and self-serving teachers unions.

SWEET FREEDOM IN *Action*

Pray for the rejuvenation of America's schools, support educational reform efforts in your community, and thank a good teacher for loving our kids.

PRINCIPLES BEFORE PARTY POLITICS
Now the Lord is the Spirit, and where the Spirit of the Lord is, there is freedom.
2 Corinthians 3:17

B ack in 2009, all across our great nation everyday Americans decided to party like it was 1773. As the Sons of Liberty pushed back against a tyrannical English king by dumping tea into Boston Harbor nearly 250 years earlier, this new crop of citizens recognized very real threats to the freedoms we cherish and decided to do something about it. Sitting idly by while watching our economy collapse, healthcare in smoking ruins, and government grow intrusively fatter just wasn't an option. Tea Partiers, with righteous fire in our bellies, determined to be heard over the cacophony of Beltway politicians who'd turned deaf ears to their constituents. No more business as usual. It was time to return to government of the people, by the people, for the people. This genuine grassroots populism had underpinnings resonating in the hearts of those who were fed up with government overreach into all aspects of our lives. We organized all across America to work together for fiscal responsibility in place of out-of-control spending, and for limited government as established by our Constitution. We've been singing sweet freedom declarations ever since this great awakening shook up the out-of-touch establishment! It is powerful!

SWEET FREEDOM IN *Action*

Today, meditate on the fact that while much work lies ahead, there is always hope for liberty. Pray that God might continue to bless America.

SLAVES AMONG US
*Defend the weak and the fatherless; uphold the cause
of the poor and the oppressed.*
Psalm 82:3

In 1818, William Wilberforce wrote: "In the Scripture, no national crime is condemned so frequently and few so strongly as oppression and cruelty...." This man of faith dedicated his life to abolishing the slave trade. Three days after Parliament abolished slavery in the British Empire, Wilberforce died.

Sadly, conditions across the globe now demand that we again take up Wilberforce's efforts.

Sex trafficking for profit is the fastest-growing criminal activity in America today. Instead of honoring and protecting women and children, exploitative predators force them into prostitution, pornography, and slavery. A significant percentage of these are very young girls. How can hearts not be grieved by this terrible injustice? Friends, we are not powerless to help victims! Research this timely topic. The more we know, the more effectively we can act.

SWEET FREEDOM IN *Action*

Today, pray for the victims of trafficking. Support faith-based organizations dedicated to abolishing it. Let's not pretend it isn't here.

AMAZING GRACE IS A SWEET SOUND
Hatred stirs up conflict, but love covers over all wrongs.
Proverbs 10:12

Wherever you look, Christians are being abused—whether it's the ridicule, marginalization, and stigmatization that Christians receive from the media and liberal elites here, or the torture, imprisonment, beheadings, and slaughter Christians suffer abroad.

So-called progressives in the West treat Christians with snobbish contempt. Radical Islamists kill us. In both cases, morality has been turned upside-down.

The Bible warns of such crumbling morality in 2 Timothy 3:2. It's all been prophesized. This passage reveals that people will be lovers of themselves, arrogant, abusive, and wicked.

The line separating right from wrong has been blurred by the worldly influences of humanism, secularism, and religious doctrines not based on the Word of God.

The outcry of the age is for "tolerance," yet how tolerant is it for people to attack Christians who simply want to live their lives by biblical principles?

The very heart of Christianity is to love our enemies, as tough as that may be. What does that love look like now that so many are labeling us "intolerant"? Our example is found in Jesus. If He showed such amazing strength and mercy in the face of horrendous treatment coming at Him, how can we, being recipients of His mercy, refuse to exercise whatever strength we can muster?

We can't refuse it. The daunting nature of required mercy and grace makes it seem impossible to implement, especially when we see hatred around us. All the more reason to tap into God's amazing grace and ask Him to show us how. He'll be delighted to teach us.

Sweet Freedom in Action

Pray to God for strength and understanding, and for the grace to endure.

THE GAMBLERS

What good is it for someone to gain the whole world,
yet forfeit their soul? Or what can anyone give
in exchange for their soul?
Mark 8:36–37

Hear the word "gambling" and I think of my dear friend, car- and truck-racing great Walker Evans. We're competitive in our fun adventures together, so inevitably we end up betting each other on the outcome of pretty much everything. Lord, forgive me if that's a sin.

You would never do *that.*

But gambling is also what we do when we run the end of a yellow light, hoping we're safe. It's when we press the pedal to the metal and hope for no flashing lights in the rearview mirror. Gambling is also what we do with our life's time and resources. We gamble with our health, our money, where we invest (somewhat like the blackjack table), and we bet we'll live long enough to make amends.

As believers, we can actually stake everything on God and what He's said. And even though we know every word is true, it may sometimes still feel like a gamble. Here's the truth. To live vibrantly like my friend Walker does, to avoid leaving this world with unrealized potential and unfulfilled dreams, we're going to have to believe that every promise God gave is ours for the taking. It's gambling on His credibility—*and winning*!

SWEET FREEDOM IN *Action*

Today, stop playing life fast and loose, hoping you won't get caught. Start trusting God—He's the safe bet.

JESUS CRACKS UP, TOO!

He will yet fill your mouth with laughter and your lips
with shouts of joy.

Job 8:21

Freedom is joy! I ordered a beautiful drawing of Jesus from the Elijah List, a great online resource for inspiration. The picture caught my attention because it shows Jesus laughing. The artist depicts Him cracking up, and *I love it*! You know He must laugh, as He's the source of true joy!

As Americans, we are born into joyous freedom. We don't know any other type of government. We cherish freedom of speech, assembly, and religion. We prize a free press and the right to bear arms. Our individual and collective freedoms are rare and sacred in this world, envied by many.

As believers, we're born again into spiritual liberty, doubly blessed by our American *and* Christian heritages. In both the founding of our country and the genesis of Christianity, great sacrifice was made for us to enjoy our liberty. Our Founding Fathers warned we must responsibly *keep* our Constitution. The Bible stirs us to *keep* God's laws.

In these difficult days, both sets of laws are a refuge, for us individually and for our nation. If we use our liberty as a license to just do as we please, we ultimately destroy its essence. More than ever, we need to be stirred to the perfect law of liberty so our nation can flourish and we can live in the fullness of God's promises.

SWEET FREEDOM IN *Action*

Today, determine to walk thankfully and carefully in all the liberty you possess. When I glance at my Jesus laughing picture, I'll remember to pray for all of you to receive divine joy and laughter, through freedom!

Open Your Home and Heart

"What no eye has seen, what no ear has heard, and what no human mind has conceived"—the things God has prepared for those who love him....
1 Corinthians 2:9

"Gals, I'm sorry for the muddy paw prints." I was a little embarrassed when a busload of Gold Star wives traveling with TAPS (Tragedy Assistance Program for Survivors) dropped by our home during their tour of Alaska. TAPS is an amazing group focusing on military widows who have lost their husbands in war, and I was honored to meet them.

My house wasn't as tidy as I would have liked, and I'd no time to prepare for their visit with home-baked treats to share. But still, graciousness exuded from every single one of these forty-three beautiful wives from all over the United States.

"That's okay," one of the ladies leaned over and whispered to me. "We've all been through much worse than paw prints on wood floors."

Hearing their stories and seeing their heroes' pictures worn on lapel buttons shamed me for sweating the small stuff. It was impossible to articulate for them America's appreciation for their sacrifices and their inspiring strength. Their husband—their life partner, their best friend, the father of their children—gave all for America, and so did these wonderful women.

Sweet Freedom in *Action*

Today, stop worrying about your house—fingerprints on windows, dust bunnies in corners, dog treats crumbled on the couch—or you may miss opening your home and heart to the people God brings you.

JESUS: HIPPIE OR WARRIOR?

Blessed are the pure in heart, for they will see God.

Matthew 5:8

The culture often paints Jesus as a long-haired, mellow hippie humming "Kumbaya" while cruising His donkey into town. I don't believe it for a minute. Scripture depicts Him as a warrior who boldly enters controversial realms for the sake of Truth.

Time and time again, Jesus publicly challenged religious leaders, politicians, and their hypocrisy. He threw the money changers out of the temple with a whip, turning over tables. Most significantly, He waged war against sin and death when He died on the cross for our sins and rose three days later. Revelation says He will return in glory on a white horse to defeat Satan in battle once and for all.

King Jesus is most certainly a triumphant warrior, but He doesn't enter battle seeking thrills or glory. Instead, having a pure heart filled with God's Truth, He exposes sin for what it is, and in the process does what no other warrior has ever done: overcome death itself.

If we follow Christ, He leads us into different battles—not against our fellow man, but against principalities and powers. John Hagee said, "A pure heart won't get us out of conflict and controversy. It may well be the very thing that gets us into it." As God sanctifies our hearts, we'll have less tolerance for sin when we see it in the world and in ourselves, because we want justice and goodness to triumph.

SWEET FREEDOM IN *Action*

Today, ask God to purify your heart, that you might see more of Him, thus becoming more like the mighty warrior Jesus.

Bite Your Tongue

Do not let any unwholesome talk come out of your mouths,
but only what is helpful for building others up according to
their needs, that it may benefit those who listen.
Ephesians 4:29

Remember your mom admonishing, "If you don't have anything nice to say, don't say anything at all"?

If only more people followed that nearly golden rule.

"I'm exercising my freedom of speech!" some insist, while spouting words that are anything but edifying.

Do you often give someone a piece of your mind? I confess to it—and most of us probably have pieces of our minds all over creation! As we grow in grace, however, we're to exercise freedom of speech more responsibly—in a manner that uplifts, rather than destroys. Even when we have to correct, even when we disagree, we can speak truth in love, and sometimes, just bite the ol' tongue and remember the song, "You say it best when you say nothing at all."

I know all about being verbally attacked. I need God's help and wisdom, sought through prayer, because left to my own devices, the words I want to speak in response may not bring edification or grace, believe me.

Sweet Freedom in *Action*

Today, remember that with freedom comes responsibility. So while you are free to say what you want, choose your words wisely, and acknowledge that sometimes it is best to say nothing at all.

SPEAK TO THE MOUNTAIN

Truly I tell you, if anyone says to this mountain,
"Go, throw yourself into the sea," and does not doubt in their
heart but believes that what they say will happen,
it will be done for them.

Mark 11:23

Speech is a skill that too many of us take for granted, something I've learned raising my son Trig, who has Down syndrome. On Trig's first day of first grade we got to hear his first "real" sentence, and we were over-the-moon excited! He announced, "No school! Me 'tay home!" Didn't matter the content, I was just so happy he strung the words together that I almost gave in and let him 'tay home to hang with me all day.

Amazing—the power of words. They're more than just sounds to hear and vibrations felt; hear them as actually being alive, used for good—or bad.

Jesus taught His disciples that whatever they spoke in faith could move mountains! Now, that's power! Do you have mountains in your life that need to be moved? Instead of speaking the obvious—"Dang, another mountain"—what would happen if we spoke *to* the mountain and told it to move? God says it'll move!

We exercise free speech for almost everything. The media utilize it to besmirch the candidate they want defeated or a celebrity they choose to mess with. Social media geeks use it to defame people they disagree with. But speech also inspires. Think about how deeply Dr. King's "I Have a Dream" speech stirs. And President Lincoln's profound and succinct Gettysburg Address. And Charlton Heston's epic NRA "from my cold, dead hands" pro-gun speech.

Jesus used speech better than anyone:

"Be healed."

"Lazarus, come forth."

"Father, forgive them."

He spoke, and things happened. *We* speak, and things happen. There's never been a more crucial time to confront mountains of adversity—poverty, debt, war, and more—and command them to move.

SWEET FREEDOM IN *Action*

Today, identify a mountain standing before you. Instead of complaining about how big and bad it is, tell it, by faith, to move. Instead of telling everyone how big your problem is, tell your problem how big your God is!

SPEAK WITH AUTHORITY

The people were amazed at his teaching, because he taught
them as one who had authority, not as the teachers of the law.
Mark 1:22

Remember those old E. F. Hutton commercials in which someone in a crowd whispered that E. F. Hutton was his broker? The whole place would stop in silence, and the narrator would say: "When E. F. Hutton talks, people listen."

Well, that's Jesus, times a trillion. Everything He did on earth demanded attention. Just His showing up changed the atmosphere. He exuded God because...He was God. It's no surprise that when He opened His mouth, He spoke with authority. We don't have a record of every word Jesus spoke, but I believe He didn't waste words, yet He didn't hold back, and He definitely didn't succumb to political correctness! Jesus spoke what was needed, when it was needed, how it was needed. Some liked it. Some didn't. No one was indifferent, and He warns us it will be that way until He returns. His words caused reaction then and now because they are infused with authority.

"Christian" means "Christ like," so aiming to model ourselves after Him, we should see every part of our day as an opportunity to make an impact—as He obviously did. Toss aside political correctness, peer pressure, conformity—as He did. That means some will like it, some will hate it.

Call things as you see them, no matter the fallout. That's what I've done. My dad was my best campaign advisor when he said, "Let Sarah be Sarah." We should all desire to speak with the authority God gives us and not try to be someone else.

SWEET FREEDOM IN *Action*

God created you as a unique individual, representing a unique aspect of Himself, the Lord of all creation. Believe in yourself, believe in your faith, and work to ensure that when you act and speak others will see and hear Christ in your words.

In Need of God's Boldness

*Now, Lord, consider their threats and enable your servants to
speak your word with great boldness.*

Acts 4:29

When the national spotlight fell on Indiana because of its Religious
Freedom Restoration Act, opponents claimed the legislation allowed
discrimination against homosexuals. That's not what the act provided,
but—as usual—the intolerant Left used bullying tactics to try to enforce
their will. Indiana's Governor Pence, a strong man of faith and a friend of
mine, had everything and the kitchen sink thrown at him until a "fix" was
offered to ease the pressure that roared all around the law.

Pressure to silence people of faith is growing fast and furious. Business
owners worry their livelihoods will be shut down. They dread being Hobby
Lobby'd or Chick-fil-A'd—demonized for taking a stand and unfairly accused
of being religious bigots. Military personnel are hassled for displaying Scripture. Chaplains are reprimanded for praying for people. Even pastors cannot
preach the tenets central to their faith without threats of retribution.

The apostles knew all about this kind of pressure. Their freedom—and
lives—were on the line, and they needed God to give them boldness to
continue speaking when it would have been safer to be silent. We, too, need
to bring our fears to God in the midst of a culture threatening our right to
speak the truths we hold dear.

Sweet Freedom in *Action*

Today, ask the Lord to grant you His boldness in the midst of fiery trials that are sure to get hotter. It's the only way to your sweet freedom.

FRIENDS OF ABE

He has made everything beautiful in its time. He has also set eternity in the human heart; yet no one can fathom what God has done from beginning to end.
Ecclesiastes 3:11

Do you remember "Friends of Bill"? As in Clinton? That was the catch-phrase used to describe the motley group of Arkansas cronies who tagged along with him to Washington, D.C., after his unlikely 1992 victory. Well, in 2005, some red-blooded Americans created a group called "Friends of Abe" (as in Lincoln) to counteract the liberalism that our culture is so eager to embrace.

And you'll never guess where that group started...

Hollywood. Yes, you read that correctly. Members are kept largely private, but some of the conservatives who aren't afraid to claim our values are actor Gary Sinise, icon Clint Eastwood, actor Kelsey Grammer, actress Patricia Heaton, actor Jon Voight, and Oscar-nominated screenwriter Lionel Chetwynd.

I love that these professionals—as well as director Nick Searcy, actress and bestselling author Suzanne Somers, singer Naomi Judd, and actresses Morgan Brittany and Janine Turner—aren't just preaching to the choir. They're boldly proclaiming conservatism in a very hostile environment.

They know if we change the culture, we change politics.

Recently, Todd and I had the honor of attending one of the Friends of Abe events at the Hilton Universal City Hotel in Los Angeles. Mark Steyn was the brilliant keynote speaker, and I had the chance to meet a lot of celebrities with common sense. (Turns out Andrew Breitbart's father-in-law is actually a hilarious comedian. I had no idea!)

Sweet Freedom in *Action*

Today, rent an Eastwood movie—I'd suggest *American Sniper*—and support conservatives in the arts.

LEGACY OF THANKSGIVING

Let the peace of Christ rule in your hearts, since as members
of one body you were called to peace. And be thankful.
Colossians 3:15

During his first administration, President Washington named Thursday, November 26, 1789, a day of Thanksgiving to "recommend to the people of the United States a day of public thanksgiving and prayer, to be observed by acknowledging with grateful hearts the many and signal favors of Almighty God."

In 1863, President Lincoln set the precedent of celebrating Thanksgiving on the last Thursday of every November, calling it "a day of Thanksgiving and Praise to our beneficent Father who dwelleth in the Heavens."

Unlike the two presidents who *recommended* Americans express gratitude, Scripture actually *commands* us to be grateful. "Be thankful" is not a suggestion; it's a mandate. Like those before us, we have been shown abundant favor, but sometimes we fail to recognize just how blessed we are. We would be wise to do what hymnist Johnson Oatman Jr. expressed in his classic hymn, "Count your blessings, name them one by one / Count your blessings, see what God has done!"

SWEET FREEDOM IN *Action*

Today, write down your reasons to be grateful. Put the list somewhere where you'll see it every day—on your bathroom mirror, on your car dashboard, near your computer mouse. Watch your attitude—and circumstances—change as you praise God with a grateful heart.

PRAISE THE LORD WITH ALL YOUR HEART
Enter his gates with thanksgiving and his courts with praise;
give thanks to him and praise his name.
Psalm 100:4

If you're like me, sometimes it feels like you've dragged your family into church, expecting the worship leader to sing just the right song and not repeat the chorus so often; and the gal behind us better sing in tune or try toning it down; and the pastor better speak just the right words to put us in a spiritual mood. God help them all if they don't! But that's backward. Psalm 100 commands us to come *into* His presence bearing a heart of gratitude, not wait for it to happen.

It's nobody's responsibility to draw it out of us; we should come before God already filled with thanksgiving, praising God even before the greeter has a chance to flash us a smile and a bulletin; even before the first note is screeched, or, er, sung.

When you encounter that person who always seems to be on top of the world, are you tempted to narrow your eyes and say, "Something's off here. No way anybody could be all happy all the time"? But a thankful heart has nothing to do with whether everything is going our way. We should express gratitude because we know what this psalmist knows: the Lord is good—regardless of what's going on in life.

SWEET FREEDOM IN *Action*

Today, quit waiting until circumstances are just right before you praise the Lord. You already have so much to thank God for, so what are you waiting for?

The Power of Nice, and *Saturday Night Live*
A gentle answer turns away wrath....
Proverbs 15:1

I was invited to be on the *Saturday Night Live* "40th Anniversary Special," which was a hoot. My date was my nephew, a stand-up comedian in NYC, who could whisper to me the names of all the actors and comedians who were around during the gig. Convenient! I guess *SNL* was capitalizing on the attention they got from a clever Tina Fey impression of me—or me of her—and thought they owed me an invitation. At the after-party, I fulfilled a promise to my nephew to meet the comedian Louis C.K. We shook hands and both sort of apologized, I because I wasn't quite sure who he was, and he because he'd said something about me that maybe wouldn't have endeared him to my mother.

Later, Louis C.K. said, "I've never in a million years apologized for anything," but he wanted to say he was sorry for some drunk tweets several years ago. He said he wasn't an "insult guy." I was blown away by his unexpected comments and kept thinking, "He didn't have to tell me that. Why is he different from the rest?"

Being in the public eye makes you vulnerable to scrutiny; it's part of the deal. On many occasions I've run into people who have trashed me or my family. But he's the first celebrity to have apologized. Maybe it surprises people, but I was sincerely humbled and appreciative. I wish I could have spoken with him longer. I did manage to invite him to Alaska to slay some salmon with us.

SWEET FREEDOM IN *Action*

Today, as the very true saying goes, be kind to everyone, for everyone is fighting some battle. Plus, making the effort to be nice might find you a friend.

GOD WRITES A FINE LIST

"Who touched me?" Jesus asked. When they all denied it,
Peter said, "Master, the people are crowding and pressing
against you." But Jesus said, "Someone touched me;
I know that power has gone out from me."
Luke 8:45–46

In our fast-paced world, we often don't take time for real people with real needs. No, we have our list of things to do, and whoever isn't on it...well, sorry. In this passage, the woman "who had been subject to bleeding for twelve years" wasn't on Jesus's list. He was en route to take care of something important. But when the woman touched Him, He stopped everything to meet the need of the one.

When I learned I was pregnant with Trig, I dreaded that certain constituents might say, "See, we elect our first woman governor, and she goes and gets herself pregnant!" And while I didn't want to slow down, learning my baby boy would have some special needs changed me as maybe nothing else has.

Jesus asked who touched Him. Well, the moment Trig was born, I knew who touched me. God specifically chose us to love His child Trig and to be compassionate toward him and others—and he is the best thing that has ever happened to our family. Trig is an example of what happens when we do slow down and let God rewrite our list of priorities, and allow others to touch our lives as we touch theirs.

SWEET FREEDOM IN *Action*

Today, let God slow you down to better appreciate His blessings.

MANAGING GOD'S MONEY

Honor the Lord with your wealth, with the firstfruits of all
your crops; then your barns will be filled to overflowing,
and your vats will brim over with new wine.
Proverbs 3:9–10

This concept of fiscal responsibility was not lost on me as governor of Alaska. That's why I used my line-item veto to cut spending by almost 10 percent. I rejected a pay raise. (As mayor, I took a voluntary pay cut.) I invested billions of dollars in state savings. I forward-funded education. See, I knew the resources were not mine to squander and that I had to do right by the people who hired me. Alaska reaped the benefits of that fiscal responsibility: during my tenure, both Standard & Poor's and Moody's upgraded Alaska's credit rating.

Our politicians in Washington should be so wise with taxpayer dollars because what's good for an individual, family, and state is also good for a nation; God's principles apply across the board. Wasteful spending that robs the American people—like $500,000 to study shrimp on a treadmill, or subsidizing the annual National Cowboy Poetry Gathering in Senator Harry Reid's state of Nevada—doesn't seem to qualify as the fiscal responsibility this Scripture describes. And funding Planned Parenthood certainly does not honor God—fiscally or morally.

SWEET FREEDOM IN *Action*

What's in your hand is not yours. It's a loan. God expects you to be obedient and wise with what He's allowed you to manage. Today, honor Him for His blessings and pray America does the same.

FINANCIAL FREEDOM

*For the Lord your God will bless you as he has promised,
and you will lend to many nations but will borrow from none.
You will rule over many nations but none will rule over you.*
Deuteronomy 15:6

God promised Israel that if they were obedient to Him, they'd lack nothing. He'd bless Israel so abundantly that they'd have plenty to lend to others. Interesting how the verse goes from not being a borrower to not being ruled. The link between indebtedness and control is reiterated in Proverbs 22:7: "The rich rule over the poor, and the borrower is slave to the lender."

America is so many trillions of dollars in debt it's almost impossible to account. Yet we have leaders refusing to acknowledge it, refusing to cut spending, and refusing to exercise fiscal prudence. What's worse is the very real danger of being owned by lenders. When we are dependent on China, a nation that does not particularly like us, we're in big trouble.

Washington spends our money in unbelievably wasteful ways. The government's backing of the green-energy company Solyndra cost us *half a billion dollars* alone! The Obama "stimulus" package, enacted in 2009, is expected to cost well over $800 billion by 2019, and the only real stimulus it has provided has been to government spending. The stories of government waste are legion. How about the $16 billion of ammunition the government purchased, only to decide it didn't need it, so it spent $1 billion to destroy it! How's that for prudently handling the nation's money and resources?

SWEET FREEDOM IN *Action*

Today, vow to pay closer attention to how politicians spend your money. Those who do not exercise fiscal restraint do not deserve your vote. Find candidates who do. Remember that bigger government is the problem, not the cure.

GOD WANTS TO BLESS THIS MESS?
A good person leaves an inheritance for their children's children, but a sinner's wealth is stored up for the righteous.
Proverbs 13:22

While Scripture teaches us the importance of giving and not hoarding our resources, it also teaches us the importance of saving to provide for our children's future—not to indulge our children, or spoil them, or leave them with a boatload of money, but as an investment to help them better themselves. That's the American Dream—of each generation sacrificing so that the next can do better. Todd and I expect our children to work hard, as our parents expected of us. Like most of you, we have had jobs since we were very young, and I'm extremely proud that our kids have amazingly admirable work ethics. But part of a good work ethic is knowing about saving money to provide for the future, including future family. We *should* take good care of children and try to leave something when we're gone. The Bible actually says those who don't provide for their own are worse than unbelievers (1 Tim. 5:8)!

Friends, the same is true of a nation. Share this with your liberal friends. Our forefathers sought to "secure the blessings of liberty" and left us an incredible legacy. The American experiment turned out to be highly successful, and with it we have every opportunity for success and prosperity. We should want to leave future generations an equal opportunity—not debt and deficits. Today's government budgets don't protect what we inherited—not one iota. We cannot expect God to bless this mess. We need to sweep our fiscal house into order as a nation, ASAP, and keep trusting that God's ways are smarter than our own.

SWEET FREEDOM IN *Action*

Today, review your family budget, pay any outstanding debts, and make sure you're saving a little every month. Get good financial advice (tune in to Dave Ramsey's radio program for that)—and get started now.

MY BROWN-EYED GIRL
Yet you, Lord, are our Father. We are the clay,
you are the potter; we are all the work of your hand.
Isaiah 64:8

When Amy Carmichael was a little girl, she hated her dark brown eyes. Every night before she went to sleep, she'd pray for God to turn her eyes to crystal-clear blue. Every morning, she'd wake up to find those same brown eyes staring back in the mirror. This was the first time young Amy realized: sometimes God says no.

Years later, she was a missionary in India. At that time, young girls were sold as "temple servants," which meant slavery, prostitution, or forced matrimony to much older men. Carmichael made it her mission to rescue these girls by going undercover. She put on a sari—traditional Indian dress—to disguise herself, and even stained her skin with coffee. Then, she'd intercept the girls on their journeys and carry them to safety ... just in the nick of time.

One day, she realized that almost no other Irish missionaries could go undercover like she could because they all had light hair and light eyes. Amy's dark brown eyes were exactly what she needed for her work!

SWEET FREEDOM IN *Action*

Today, remember that every little detail has a purpose, even the parts of your physical appearance that you don't like. Instead of being unhappy with the way God made you, remember that you were intentionally designed by a loving God. He knows what's best for you.

NATIONAL ENQUIRER–WORTHY WORLD

But he said to me, "My grace is sufficient for you, for my
power is made perfect in weakness." Therefore I will boast
all the more gladly about my weaknesses, so that Christ's
power may rest on me.
2 Corinthians 12:9

At one point when Hillary Clinton was U.S. secretary of state, the media started buzzing about how "tired and withdrawn" she looked, attending official meetings with no more than a quick stroke of lipstick.

I know the feeling.

The paparazzi once busted me leaving a hot yoga class *sans* makeup. I admit it. I looked like h*ll because I'd just come from a workout hotter than hell. My photo took the cover of a tabloid's "Look How Bad They Look in Real Life" edition. Whatever.

A fantastic aspect of living in faith is comfort in admitting shortcomings. I don't have to get another degree, or hold another office, or weigh what it says on my driver's license, or be perfectly coiffed to be perfectly loved. Granted, I'm a believer in "when the barn needs painting, paint it!" But even when we're looking a mess, God is good to us. He actually takes our weaknesses and uses them for His glory! Thank you, God. They're good for something.

How incredible is that?

Like Rick Warren said, "If God only used perfect people, nothing would get done. God will use anybody if you're available."

As faithful Christians, we can relax, be vulnerable, show others our imperfections, be honest about our weaknesses, and realize that all that we accomplish clearly comes from the grace of our Heavenly Father.

SWEET FREEDOM IN *Action*

Today, trust God to use the whole messy package that is you for His glory.

DEEP ROOTS

*They will be like a tree planted by the water that sends out
its roots by the stream. It does not fear when heat comes; its
leaves are always green. It has no worries in a year of drought
and never fails to bear fruit.*

Jeremiah 17:8

Often we remember from childhood a favorite tree we climbed, played on, hid in and around...memorable because it was consistently dependable and sturdy. The Northwest is known for mighty evergreens, prized for durability, usefulness, and beauty. Every time I hike beneath their branches or marvel at their ability to hold tons of snow, I'm reminded of this verse. God calls His people to be like the strong tree, firmly planted in the soil of His Truth and bearing His fruit.

We need to have deep roots in our faith—that means study and prayer.

We also need to flower like the tree—to show our faith in the practice of our lives, to be an example of wonder to others.

And we need to be sturdy in our faith—when hit by the winds and rains and lightning of doubters and deceivers we might bend ever so slightly by sheer force of the storm, but we'll never break.

SWEET FREEDOM IN *Action*

Vow to ensure, through prayer, study, and practice, that your faith is as sturdy as that memorable old tree from your childhood.

CRINGEWORTHY WORDS: "I HAVE EVOLVED"

This is what the Lord commands: When a man makes a vow to the Lord or takes an oath to obligate himself by a pledge, he must not break his word but must do everything he said.
Numbers 30:1–2

Promises made, contributions accepted, votes counted. The newly elected are sworn in, then sworn at. Why? Because some politicians' actions in office contradict campaign promises. Bad enough. But it becomes truly cringeworthy when they attempt to legitimize these broken promises with these three words: "I have *evolved*." This gives public service a bad name.

With today's complicit media condoning their favored ones' flip-flops while condemning citizens who hold them accountable, more than ever Newt Gingrich's words ring true: "The destructive, vicious, negative nature of much of the news media makes it harder to govern this country, *harder to attract decent people to run for office.*"

But "decent people" know they have an obligation—a duty—to serve regardless of media double standards. Luke 12 tells us, "From everyone who has been given much, much will be demanded; and from the one who has been entrusted with much, much more will be asked." Being an American gives us an automatic head start in this world. Be thankful for it, and do something with it.

SWEET FREEDOM IN *Action*

Each of us has a role to play in making this a better nation, whether it's by serving in the military, holding public office, or even supporting a worthy charity. Whatever you are called to do, do it, get involved, do something for America, and be true to God by staying true to your word—and His!

ROCK AND ROLL AIN'T (ALWAYS) NOISE POLLUTION

I tell you, whoever publicly acknowledges me before others, the
Son of Man will also acknowledge before the angels of God.
Luke 12:8

Ted Nugent is the boldest, baddest rocker on the planet. This iconic Michigander isn't preaching to the choir, and if church people can't respect his energetic, effective walk with God then they don't get today's Scripture. Nugent infiltrates pop culture in influential ways most of us can only dream of, and his public acknowledgment of faith puts him on the side of the angels.

You won't be salt and light in a hurting world if you don't use your God-given talents. To reflect His light, don't close the door on His unorthodox ways of meeting people exactly where they are today—even in Motor City mosh pits.

When I run, I've got Gene Simmons, Alice Cooper, Madison Rising, and many more on my iTunes playlist. Some might think these singers are "out there." But shouldn't these hard-rocking, faith-filled conservatives be used for God's ultimate purpose? (I've met these guys. I dare you to tell them differently.)

There must be something in that Detroit water, because Nugent's buddy there in Michigan, Kid Rock, is another one acknowledging in song the Good Book's guidance for those who may not hear it any other way. I've got his song "Jesus and Bocephus" on repeat—"I went from Jim Beam, to my Bible / With Jesus and Bocephus, right there by my side."

Today, listen to a song from one of my friends above, and thank God they're using the talents He gave them. We should all do as much. Vow to use what talents God has given you.

GRIDIRON WISDOM FOR THE AGES

...so that your faith might not rest on human wisdom, but on God's power.

1 Corinthians 2:5

This verse applies to every cultural challenge today. Thank God He knows us so well that He kept His instructions simple so there'd be no question: every single solution we seek is explained there in black and white, in His Word.

My nephew-in-law is a literal giant of a young man, a rugged, handsome former USC offensive lineman. We call him "Thor." He sent me this verse after we discussed man's "wisdom" always being used to justify sin. It is the wisdom of man that tells us to just accept worldliness, political corruption, selfishness... insert here your own observations. Within man is a God-shaped hole. If we fill it with our own superficial understandings instead of the life-changing wisdom and power of the Holy Spirit, we'll live in confusion and hopelessness.

SWEET FREEDOM IN *Action*

Today, put your faith in God's wisdom. Read His Word in Holy Scripture. Practice His tenets in your life. Worship Him and give Him thanks in prayer at home and at church. It takes a humble bow to Christ to acknowledge need of His wisdom in place of our own, but if the mighty "Thor" can take a knee for the Lord, you can too.

PREPARING A PLACE

Do not let your hearts be troubled. You believe in God;
believe also in me. My Father's house has many rooms; if that
were not so, would I have told you that I am going there
to prepare a place for you? And if I go and prepare a place for
you, I will come back and take you to be with me that you also
may be where I am.
John 14:1–3

If you're like me, you scrub the house like a madman when the whole tribe comes over. I prepare for them: shoveling the driveway, cooking foods *I've* been craving (using it as an excuse to bake my girlfriend's famous oatmeal raisin cookies), tying up work's loose ends, etc. We prepare for family and friends because we love them and want them to enjoy! That's exactly what God is doing for us—preparing a place. Jesus lets us know that He is preparing a place for us because He wants us, His faithful disciples, to be with Him.

We don't get to choose our families—except for our spouse—but we do get to *choose* to have a personal relationship with Jesus, to love Him, to follow Him…all the way to heaven. When we decide to make Him Lord of our lives, only then will that place be prepared for us in His kingdom.

SWEET FREEDOM IN *Action*

Rest assured Jesus is preparing a place for you in His heavenly kingdom. Vow today to be His worthy disciple.

WHEN IT RAINS, HIS GRACE POURS

I know that my redeemer lives, and that in the end....
I will see God....
Job 19:25–26

With so much bad news in the world, it's easy to think that things are just going to keep getting worse and worse.

But I doubt that God wants us to think that way.

In the 1970s, America went through a gloomy period. But with the presidency of Ronald Reagan it became "morning in America" once again. Reagan was a realist, but he was also an optimist because he had faith in God's Providence, and so should we.

God tells us that in the end we will see Him, which means if we are faithful nothing can stand between us and our heavenly glory. From God's Word to your heart, cling to the promise that "God works for the good of those who love Him, who have been called according to His purpose" (Rom. 8:28).

God never forsakes us. That's one lesson from the book of Job. If we stay faithful through all of life's trials, God will reward us in the end. We should always trust in His justice.

SWEET FREEDOM IN *Action*

Today, no matter what difficulties you're going through, put your trust in God—He'll always be there for you.

EXPERIENCE THE RAINBOW

*And God said, "This is the sign of the covenant I am making
between me and you and every living creature with you, a covenant
for all generations to come: I have set my rainbow in the clouds,
and it will be the sign of the covenant between me and the earth.
Whenever I bring clouds over the earth and the rainbow appears
in the clouds, I will remember my covenant between me and you
and all living creatures of every kind. Never again will the waters
become a flood to destroy all life. Whenever the rainbow appears
in the clouds, I will see it and remember the everlasting covenant
between God and all living creatures of every kind on the earth."
So God said to Noah, "This is the sign of the covenant I have
established between me and all life on the earth."*
Genesis 9:12–17

There's just something about a rainbow! The first one appeared after
Noah and his family emerged from the horrifying experience of the
worldwide flood, and it was a sign of God's beneficence and His trust in
Noah. Today, people still marvel at the beauty of a rainbow.

It remains a sign that after every storm and flood in our own lives,
there is a rainbow, there is salvation waiting for us in God's mercy. We
should be as excited about that mercy as that man in the YouTube video
marveling at the rainbow.

SWEET FREEDOM IN *Action*

Today, view your trials as preparation for the next phase of life God is drawing you toward, and be thankful for His promises.

PUT UP YOUR DUKES

Fight the good fight of the faith. Take hold of the eternal
life to which you were called when you made your good
confession in the presence of many witnesses.

1 Timothy 6:12

In polite society, people don't like to think about "fighting." Instead, they tend toward dialogue and conversation. The mellow mantra is, "Don't get angry, don't get riled up. Use your words." Oh, kumbaya.

Notice the language above. "Fight the good fight of the faith." Don't dialogue it. Don't talk about it. Don't blog it. *Fight for it!*

What does that mean? It's pretty simple. Know what pleases God, and stick with those convictions. Never allow fear or intimidation to cause you to back down from what you know is right. Sure, standing up for what we believe in comes with costs. We might be rejected socially for violating political correctness. We might be punished for things like displaying the American flag where someone doesn't like it. Or we might be sued for exercising our First Amendment rights to freedom of conscience and religion. But remember that the Lord rewards every man for his righteousness and his faithfulness (1 Sam. 26:23).

SWEET FREEDOM IN *Action*

Today, put up your dukes and decide to fight for your faith.

LET YOUR LIGHT SHINE, HALLELUJAH

In the same way, let your light shine before others, that they
may see your good deeds and glorify your Father in heaven.
Matthew 5:16

"Hide it under a bushel? No! I'm going to let it shine."
During a certain era, every child who grew up in church sang
"This Little Light of Mine, I'm Going to Let It Shine." When we sang it,
our finger was the candle, our cupped hand the darkening bushel.

We can recite something so often, using such familiar words, that we
fail to understand its underlying meaning and then apply it to life.

Here goes.

People can see in us a light that magnifies our oneness with God
through our words and deeds. We don't expect to be praised for any good
thing we may do. Instead, we roll up our sleeves with humility and try to
do more of it as we seek to honor God. Just as we would place a light on a
lamp stand to illuminate a room, we should try to shine bright by our
example.

SWEET FREEDOM IN *Action*

Today, what bushel hides or dims your light? Pray that God helps you
reflect His light, shining especially on those who are hurting.

RICHES TO RAGS

A little sleep, a little slumber, a little folding of the hands to rest—and poverty will come on you like a thief and scarcity like an armed man.

Proverbs 24:33–34

P roverbs tells us that "idle hands are the devil's workshop," and it warns that unless we are diligent, unless we work hard, unless we look after our material well-being, poverty can come upon us like a "thief"; material scarcity can come upon us like an "armed man."

Sloth is one of the seven deadly sins in the Bible. And it's not just that lack of effort can lead to material poverty, but to spiritual poverty as well.

As Americans we have been born into a land of opportunity. We should be thankful for that opportunity, and we should wake up every day looking to make the most of it—to better ourselves, our family, our nation.

America, if she is to survive, has to be a nation of doers.

SWEET FREEDOM IN *Action*

Today, wake up! Get up! Strive to be ambitious in every area of life so that you will reap the rewards of your labor, both on earth and in heaven.

PEACE OF MIND

For God is not a God of disorder but of peace—
as in all the congregations of the Lord's people.
1 Corinthians 14:33

Peace can often be hard to come by. In a span of a few weeks I had a beloved pet die, a cancer scare, legal battles with nefarious characters (including my daughters' stalkers), flooding in our house, two friends die in freak accidents, and more additional calamities than I care to remember. Of course, others have gone through much worse than what I went through in those weeks. Life can certainly be hard or challenging, and when you're in those circumstances it's all too easy to feel overwhelmed, or at the end of your rope, or even self-pitying. The last thing you're likely thinking about is trying to bless others. But that's what we should be thinking about.

Take a look at Christ. Jesus knew His death was imminent and that only *He* had the power to confer peace upon His followers. Instead of wallowing in His own justifiable angst, He comforted others.

After explaining to His followers why He had to leave, He not only promised that He would return, but He also assured them that the Holy Spirit would come to comfort, teach, and guide them. In the same way, we are assured that same peace if we truly trust in God's redemptive plan for us and are obedient to His Word.

SWEET FREEDOM IN *Action*

Remember this today: "I have told you these things, so that in me you may have peace. In this world you will have trouble. But take heart! I have overcome the world" (John 16:33).

GOODNESS IN THE LAND OF THE LIVING

*I remain confident of this: I will see the goodness of the Lord
in the land of the living.*
Psalm 27:13

When I was a child, my idea of heaven was my own room, away from my sisters.

As an adult, my heavenly aspirations have shifted a bit. Now that I've lived long enough to have friends and loved ones pass away, I sometimes catch myself thinking about reconnecting with them in heaven one day. That alone is enough to make heaven amazing. Seeing my loved ones again, in a place far more exquisite than even Alaska, is something to look forward to.

But along with heavenly hopes, we're able to enjoy God's goodness while still on earth. The psalmist wrote that he was "confident" of this.

SWEET FREEDOM IN *Action*

Don't be content to wait for heavenly glories. Instead, strengthen yourself in prayer and Bible reading and blessing others. Expect to see God's goodness right where you are, even today.

HATERS GONNA HATE, SO SAYETH ME
Whoever heeds discipline shows the way to life,
but whoever ignores correction leads others astray.
Proverbs 10:17

Constructive criticism = fine. But unwarranted, unhelpful reproof? Not so much.

Abe Lincoln shut out unconstructive criticism and distractions to accomplish the task at hand: "If I...listen to every criticism, let alone act on them, then this shop may as well be closed for all other businesses. I...do my best, and if the end result is good, then I do not care for any criticism, but if the end result is not good, then even the praise of ten angels would not make the difference." Criticized for his looks, lack of education, and lowly upbringing, he taught that we mustn't let the critics get us down or rob us of our confidence. He said, "It's nothing but a noise!'"

Push past that noise.

Remember: unjust critics tear down; they don't create. It's easier to criticize than to lead. Teddy Roosevelt wrote: "It is not the critic who counts.... The credit belongs to the man who is actually in the arena...who strives valiantly; who errs, who comes up short again and again...but...who spends himself for a worthy cause; who at best knows in the end the triumph of high achievement, and who, at the worst, if he fails, at least he fails while daring greatly...."

Dare greatly! Spend yourself for a worthy cause!

SWEET FREEDOM IN *Action*

Today, when you feel discouraged and criticized, heed my dad's favorite advice: "Don't retreat, just reload!"

BUT GIRLY MEN CAN OVERCOME, TOO

But when I stumbled, they gathered in glee;
assailants gathered against me without my knowledge.
They slandered me without ceasing.

Psalm 35:15

"Today is the sort of day where the sun only comes up to humiliate you."

My manly nephews, cousins, and sons recited this line from *Fight Club* during a mass wrestling match at our family reunion. But the thought is deep; it taught me something.

Light exposes darkness. Justice exposes evil. The world hates its sins being exposed by the better example of the righteous. If you live with a smile on your face and goodwill in your heart, people will condemn you as a goody two-shoes. If you present people with uncomfortable truths, they might shout and bluster and change the subject. If you say that Jesus forgives sin, people might hate you for implying that there is even such a thing as sin.

Don't think that just because you speak the truth people will readily accept it. Sinners, and that includes all of us, have a million reasons not to accept the truth. It takes grace—and, yes, effort—to stay faithful and keep the truth in front of us.

Since we're only human, we slip. Some days maybe it's just a smidgen, but our culture today doesn't want to encourage virtue; it wants to see virtue do a face-plant. So the pattern is predictable: Christians mess up, then they are discredited, humiliated, and discarded. Try as we might, justified or not, we *will* in some metaphorical way be crucified for following Christ. But we're all in this together—stay strong and lean into one another for fight club–like determination.

SWEET FREEDOM IN *Action*

One of my nephews quoted an often-repeated expression: "Adversity introduces a man to himself." Reflect on how the adversity in your own life can be turned to good through God's grace.

FROM AN OPPRESSIVE MARCH TO DANCING FREE

*Let us not become weary in doing good, for at the proper time
we will reap a harvest if we do not give up.*

Galatians 6:9

If you're an American patriot who wants to restore constitutional government to our land, who wants to see big government cut back to its rightful small-government boundaries, who wants a nation once again united under the banner of faith and freedom...well, we know we've got our work cut out for us. We may have big challenges ahead, but name me a generation that didn't. There's nothing wrong with America that our activism and some good old-fashioned election victories can't fix.

Elections are where we the people can fire politicians who don't abide by the Constitution; who don't support liberty, or the right to life, or the right of an entrepreneur to follow his dream, start a business, and create jobs unhindered by burdensome regulation and crushing taxes.

Our mission is to take back our government so that it once again represents a land not of government subsidies and patronage and welfare dependency, but of individual spirit, drive, and initiative; not of government direction but of individual responsibility; not of tax-fed bureaucrats but of businesses meeting real market needs and creating jobs.

SWEET FREEDOM IN *Action*

Patriotism, like faith, is for the long haul. We should never be discouraged, because God is always with us; and this is America, where anything is possible! Don't give up!

SPORTS ARE A METAPHOR
And let us run with perseverance the race marked out for us.
Hebrews 12:1

A favorite writer of mine, Dr. George Sheehan, was a runner. He explained how in an endurance race, cheering supporters can ease your way. Just when things seem like they're at their worst and you're going to die, you round the corner, and maybe someone's there cheering you on.

But that's not where you show what you're made of. Real "inner strength" shows up when no one's looking, when no one's cheering.

To reach your goals in all things, you must put in tough, drudging, thankless, lonely miles. God urges us to do it even when it's hard. Especially when it's hard! He promises that when it seems like you can't take another step, there's a hidden reservoir of strength to draw upon to endure and finish well. Some call this personal resolve. I call it an appreciated free gift of the Holy Spirit. Whatever you call it, it resides in all of us. When you need it most, it will be there.

When you reach a goal, be it in sports, business, or family, it makes you *stronger* and it is *satisfying*, especially if it was achieved amid particularly tough circumstances. Margaret Thatcher said, "Look at a day when you are supremely satisfied at the end. It's not a day when you lounge around doing nothing; it's when you've had everything to do and you've done it."

SWEET FREEDOM IN *Action*

Today, push yourself! Exhaust yourself. There is great joy in finding out what you're made of! God blesses your effort, especially if you go the extra mile.

INNER STRENGTH

With flattery he will corrupt those who have violated the covenant, but the people who know their God will firmly resist him.

Daniel 11:32

One of the dangers of democracy is politicians flattering "the people," telling them popular lies to get elected and stay elected. A lot of politicians will say anything to get your vote, just as some salesmen will say anything to make a sale, or a person with bad intentions will say anything to lead you astray.

In the words of that old country song, "You've got to stand for something or you'll fall for anything." Sure, it's possible for a politician, like anyone else, to be confronted with new facts or new ideas and legitimately change his mind. But I think all of us have an instinctive wariness about flip-flopping. It might indicate a politician with no real convictions or courage, merely self-interest.

As people of faith, we're people of conviction and of honesty. We know what we believe, and we should know better than to let a smooth-talking politician, salesman, or partner flatter us into overlooking the truth. The greatest strength we can have is not in our muscles, but in our souls. We need inner strength not to be corrupted by those who would flatter us and deceive us.

SWEET FREEDOM IN *Action*

Trust your core convictions, and pray that God might strengthen you to always see through deceivers, to keep your eyes on what is right, and to stay faithful and honest and true.

NEVER FORSAKEN

My God, my God, why have you forsaken me?
Why are you so far from saving me, so far from my
cries of anguish?
Psalm 22:1

Give credit to the Bible, it doesn't sugarcoat things. God recognizes our misery. He recognizes that we often suffer from injustices. He knows that we can feel lonely and forgotten, or worse, persecuted and abused. He sent the apostles out into the world, and they were martyred. Christians today are often mocked. In other parts of the world they are being targeted and killed for their faith. He knows our life can be a trail of tears—and yet...

God gave His only begotten Son that we might be saved. He partook of our humanity so that He would know, as intimately as possible, what it means to be human, to endure suffering, even to die horribly. And yet....

And yet, with God there is always hope. The Creator is also the Savior. We will have days when we cry in anguish. We will have days when we feel alone. We will have days of grief and suffering. But God is always with us. He always cares for us. In the end, He will make things right.

SWEET FREEDOM IN *Action*

Pray that you might always cherish a sense of the immediate presence of God. We are never alone—never. Reach out to God in prayer and give thanks for His faithfulness.

WAR IS HELL

Praise be to the Lord my Rock, who trains my hands for war,
my fingers for battle.
Psalm 144:1

"War is the most damnably bad thing," Oswald Chambers said. "Because God overrules a thing and brings good out of it does not mean that the thing itself is a good thing...."

It is said that "old men declare wars, and send young men to fight them." That gives those "old men" a serious moral obligation to declare war only when absolutely necessary for our own self-defense. War should be a last resort. War should not be about foreign "nation building"—that's not our job, and it's naïve to think that we can "build" another nation. When we go to war, it has to be for a definable, achievable end, and because war is required to protect the United States and our closest allies.

If we commit American troops, the sons and daughters of tear-stained parents, often young fathers and mothers themselves, it had darn well better be necessary.

Sadly, we know that war is sometimes *still* necessary, which is why we, as Americans, must always have the best-led and the best-equipped army in the world. War is an unfortunate fact of life, and we must always be ready for it, just as we should always be prayerful about deterring war, hoping to achieve peace through our strength.

SWEET FREEDOM IN *Action*

Today, vow to stay educated on matters of foreign policy and to vote for leaders who know that peace comes through strength and that if war comes, there is, as General Douglas MacArthur said, no substitute for victory.

I'M IN THE LORD'S ARMY, YES SIR

David left Gath and escaped to the cave of Adullam....
All those who were in distress or in debt or discontented
gathered around him, and he became their commander.
About four hundred men were with him.
1 Samuel 22:1–2

I think we can all identify with David in "the cave of Adullam." We've all had times in our lives when we wanted to hide in a cave, hoping somehow life would change. But like David, we learn that there really is no place to hide.

Funny how God works. He sent guys who were in distress, in debt, and discontent to that cave, and David became commander over them. It was one motley crew. David might have doubted whether he would be able to do much with them. Yet, these were the very warriors described in 1 Chronicles 12 as "brave warriors, ready for battle and able to handle the shield and spear. Their faces were the faces of lions, and they were as swift as gazelles in the mountains...."

If you doubt you're good enough to be used by God, you don't know God. He loves to take ordinary folks—think Moses with his stutter—and do extraordinary things with them. Though those men came to David in less than ideal circumstances, they didn't leave that way. God used their ordinary lives to accomplish His extraordinary purpose.

SWEET FREEDOM IN *Action*

Remember the rallying cry of Charles Spurgeon: "Bankrupt debtors make good soldiers for the King! Come, then, without more ado, and be enlisted in the King's army!" God wants us in His army, whatever our circumstances, whatever our debts, whatever our merit. Let's go!

JUDGE NOT, OR SIMPLE READING COMPREHENSION?
Do not judge, and you will not be judged…
Luke 6:37

It rarely fails. When a Christian speaks out about anything, someone pipes up with, "Judge not, lest ye be judged."

People who've never darkened the door of a church know that one by heart. But most of the time, those reciting this verse with the ardor of a priest are confused about what "being judgmental" really is.

For example, calling out a bank robber or a tax fraud isn't a matter of "being judgmental." It's a matter of being able to read "thou shalt not steal" and apply it to the situation. There are certain activities that are laid out in the Bible as sins—Revelation 21:8 has a sobering list.

To believe the Bible and call these activities "sins" is certainly not a case of being overly "judgmental."

Instead, it's pretty basic—just reading comprehension.

SWEET FREEDOM IN *Action*

Today, reflect on our responsibility to always tell the truth—including calling a sin a sin.

THE FRUIT TEST
By their fruit you will recognize them.
Matthew 7:16

I once knew a woman who made the room brighter just by leaving it. She was a local politician with whom I tried to work for years before finally giving up. Then, life became sweeter. When she was around, tension in the air seemed to rise. She was just so doggone miserable, she found everything to complain about. After watching her manipulate people around her, causing all to be in a discontented state, I ended obligatory interactions with the Debbie Downer *because it was bringing me down.*

While no one but God knows whether a person's soul will end up in heaven or hell, today's passage shows that we actually *should judge* actions, and goes on to say, "A good tree cannot bear bad fruit, and a bad tree cannot bear good fruit." That's pretty simple. Call it the "fruit test."

If a person is full of gossip and strife and seems to cause discontent, it's good to recognize they're bearing bad fruit. This recognition is called discernment, and we're called to practice it. It's also called using your head for something other than a hat rack.

When you recognize that a relationship is a bad one, shake its dust from your feet and move on.

SWEET FREEDOM IN *Action*

Today, apply the "fruit test" to people and situations in your life. When deliberating whether to continue a relationship, ask, "Does it bear good fruit?" Act accordingly and confidently.

Just a Minute

*A thousand years in your sight are like a day that has
just gone by, or like a watch in the night.*

Psalm 90:4

Heard the one about the boy who asked how long a million minutes was to God?

"Oh, son, a million minutes is like just one minute to me!"

"Wow! What about a million dollars, God?"

"Child, a million dollars is just one penny!"

"Okay then, God—may I have a penny?!"

"Of course, precious son!" God promised. "In a minute."

Do you ever feel like you're waiting on God to provide, and He just isn't hearing? Like your self-established deadline has come and gone without a peep from the Almighty?

You're not alone. We scratch our heads as God seems to take His precious time. But it actually *is* HIS time. He created it. He's above it.

The good news? The incredible riches of the kingdom of heaven are worth whatever wait God imposes. And, indeed, He knows best. He provides according to His will more than we ever ask or imagine.

The immeasurable gifts of God are available in a divinely appointed time. It has to fit into His blueprint for your life; it's guaranteed to be perfect timing.

Sweet Freedom in *Action*

Today, stop fretting about when your prayer will be answered, and realize that, with faith, your prayer will be answered when the time is right.

HEDGING HEAVEN'S BET

Then he said, "Jesus, remember me when you come into your kingdom." Jesus answered him, "Truly I tell you, today you will be with me in paradise."
Luke 23:42–43

As Jesus was dying on the cross, He had a thief on either side of Him. One of them mocked Jesus and the other one asked Him to be remembered when Jesus went to heaven. At that very moment, that split second, when the thief asked to be remembered, he was saved. Jesus listened to his plea and assured him that he would be with Him in paradise. This guy didn't have to prove himself to Jesus; he didn't have to pray a flowery prayer. He simply asked to be with Jesus. Wonder what was going through the mind of this thief? What a relief it had to be to know he'd be in heaven! The thought of being in heaven with Jesus, the King of Kings, should keep us hopeful, however dark our days. The thief knew where he wanted to spend eternity and humbly asked for it. Thank God our Father lets us do the same.

SWEET FREEDOM IN *Action*

Just like the thieves, we need to make a choice: either to live life with God or without Him. No matter how enticing culture tries to make the alternative, I've always seen it as the better bet to believe in and trust in God.

I Can't Do Everything, But I Can Do Everything I Can

He said to them, "Go into all the world and
preach the gospel to all creation."
Mark 16:15

The topic of evangelism can be scary because we sometimes think we have to go into the rugged, dangerous areas of the world as missionaries in order to effectively share the Good News of Christ. But there is plenty of domestic missionary work to be done here in America, spreading the Gospel, caring for the unwanted, and helping the poor and the struggling. Not everyone is called to be a missionary overseas.

As Christians, we should also share the Gospel message in word and live it in action. We know that we can't do everything, but we can do everything we can. We're all called in unique ways to "go into all the world and preach the Gospel." Maybe that means hacking through Guatemalan jungles to meet a community's medical need, installing water purification systems on an Indian reservation, or rebuilding an Eskimo village's burned-down schoolhouse. Or it could mean something closer to home, like contributing to crisis pregnancy or hospice care centers. No matter how big or small, we can *all* do something.

Sweet Freedom in *Action*

Today, reflect on how you can be the best evangelist. It might be donating to a foreign mission. It might be helping others become missionaries. Or it just might be that time in your life when you feel called to traverse foreign jungles, scorched deserts, or frozen tundra to offer a hand to those in need. Whatever you're called to do, don't just think about it—*do* it!

THANKING GOD FOR FOOD WHEN YOUR PANTRY IS EMPTY
Open wide your mouth and I will fill it.
Psalm 81:10

In 1836, George Mueller, the pastor of a small church in England, saw homeless children on the streets. He wanted to do something for them, but he and his wife couldn't afford to take care of so many children in their rented home.

Instead of giving up on the idea, Mueller decided to pray. For everything. He prayed for a building, for chairs, for a certain number of beds, and for books. You name it, God provided it all, and the Muellers began an orphanage.

One day, the housemother told Mueller they'd run out of food. He calmly instructed the children to sit at the table. He took their hands and thanked God for breakfast...in a house without food! Then, they waited.

Soon, they heard a knock at the door. It was a baker. For some reason, he felt like they would need bread. So, he got up early to bake several batches for them. Just as they were about to eat, he heard another knock. The milkman! His cart had collapsed in front of their orphanage and the milk would spoil before he could repair his wheel. He then brought in ten huge jugs of milk—exactly the amount they needed.

The Muellers went on to take care of more than ten thousand orphans over the years.

SWEET FREEDOM IN *Action*

Today, know that God cares about all of your specific needs. Don't be afraid to cast every worry on Him. He's asking for it! He'll take care of you.

SEND ME

Then I heard the voice of the Lord saying, "Whom shall I send?
And who will go for us?" And I said, "Here am I. Send me!"
Isaiah 6:8

The song "Here I Am" by Down Here says, "Here I am, somehow my story is a part of your plan."

That's a good reminder that we're called to accomplish something for God—even if we don't know what.

But we can learn, as our life story unfolds. Each season adds experience that can help us help others.

When we step forward to say, "Lord, send me!" we shouldn't look for the easiest or most glamorous opportunities to serve.

We're put where we are for a reason and our call from Christ might be very near at hand: to wipe the nose of a child, to sit up at night helping with homework, or to talk with a lonely, elderly relative. Joyce Meyer says, "It's amazing to me the number of people who will volunteer to help at church but won't lift a finger to help at home!"

Big testimonies—sometimes *the biggest*—come through the little things, how we handle the simple chores of our lives. We need to live every day, every moment, as a missionary sent by Christ, even if we're only cleaning up the yard.

SWEET FREEDOM IN *Action*

Today, resolve to live a life of service to those around you, remembering that your life story is part of God's plan.

MEET THEM WHERE THEY ARE

*To the weak I became weak, to win the weak. I have become
all things to all people so that by all possible means I might
save some. I do all this for the sake of the gospel, that I may
share in its blessings.*
1 Corinthians 9:22–23

To be successful in politics and in business you need to find common ground with the voter and the customer. Fail that and you won't succeed. The same is true when we act as witnesses for Christ. We need to meet people where they are. That means being gracious—grace-filled—and not trying to bully people or shame them.

I once had a politician pin his lapel button on my chest (without my permission) on live TV. Let me tell you, I wasn't impressed by that.

No one wants to be bullied into something, not even something that could save their life, as a life of faith actually does.

And few people want to be argued into it.

If a person comes up to you and asks constructive questions about the faith, that's great. And if you don't have the answers, help them find somebody who does. Constructive questions mean an intellectual curiosity and openness to the truth. Heated arguments, on the other hand, rarely end well.

Paul tells us that we must *share* the blessings of faith; and the best way to share the faith is by the humble and diplomatic witness of your life. There are a lot of people out there, hollow and hurting, who will want what you have—the serenity and confidence of faith.

SWEET FREEDOM IN *Action*

Today, remember that sharing the faith doesn't mean we have to stand on a street corner with a megaphone. Our better witness is to live an openly Christian life of kindness and service.

RETURN BAD FRUIT
Thus, by their fruit you will recognize them.
Matthew 7:20

This Scripture applies to politicians as well as anyone.

What really amazes me, though, is how little this wisdom ever gets applied.

Liberal policies in this country can be linked directly to an almost unbelievable breakdown of the traditional family, to a corruption of our culture to the point that it's often unwise to leave a child at home with the television remote control (that wasn't a problem when I was a kid), to a national debt of astronomical proportions that will burden Americans for generations to come, to a heightening of racial division and racial politics, to rising crime and attacks on police, to welfare dependency, to bureaucrats who snip away at our freedom, to attempts to weaken our military...really, the list of evils that can legitimately be linked to liberal policies is endless.

And yet liberals keep pushing the same snake oil of big government, high taxes, foreign policy weakness, an apparently endless sexual revolution, and cowardly political correctness, and all too often they get elected.

Part of that is because too many people like us don't pay enough attention. We don't look at the fruits of feel-good, sound-good policies. And a lot of the time we don't even vote.

The Left wants to fundamentally transform America—that means to take us away from our Christian and constitutional principles. I don't know about you, but I like the fruits of our Founding Fathers' ideals that are based on time-tested truths and have proved to be infinitely better than the fruits of modern liberalism.

Today, resolve to vote elected representatives bearing bad fruit out of office. That's your right!

ISOLATE, INSULATE, AND ELIMINATE

The thief comes only to steal and kill and destroy;
I have come that they may have life, and have it to the full.
John 10:10

In this Scripture, the "thief" is Satan. And what does he do? He steals, kills, and destroys. Be watchful and on guard.

His plan is to isolate you first from the plan God has for you and the people in your life. If something horrible happens, it's our human nature to want to retreat and wallow in self-pity. The next step in the devil's plan is to insulate you. This means he wants to keep you enslaved to your less-than-ideal situation. He wants to keep you away from anyone or anything that would feed your spirit—for example, the Church. The last and most terrible part of Satan's plan is to eliminate you. This can be literal or figurative. To eliminate one's self is to turn away from God completely, and that's exactly what Satan wants you to do. This is not living abundantly; this is not God's plan for your life.

SWEET FREEDOM IN *Action*

If you've gone through something hard and you feel yourself pulling away (isolating) from the Body of Christ, stop and reevaluate. Reach out to a church and get help. Start living the life God intends for you— one that is abundant!

TAKE YOUR POSITION

Though the fig tree does not bud and there are no grapes on the vines, though the olive crop fails and the fields produce no food, though there are no sheep in the pen and no cattle in the stalls, yet I will rejoice in the Lord, I will be joyful in God my Savior.
Habakkuk 3:17–18

When things seem to be going wrong in our lives, how often do we forget to still rejoice in the Lord?

Quite a lot, I bet.

The prophet Habakkuk reminds us to trust in God, no matter what; to know that there is a divine plan, that things happen for a reason, that even when evil men triumph, it is for a season, and that ultimately justice will be delivered by God.

Habakkuk is no passive observer. He questions God. He seeks answers. He finds them in faithfulness.

Our faith will always be challenged by circumstances, by the ways of the world, but we are called not just to loyalty to God, but to rejoice in His mercy, His grace, His plan, and His gift of our lives. We owe Him everything.

SWEET FREEDOM IN  *Action*

Be like Habakkuk and rejoice in the Lord. God will never abandon us; we should always be faithful to Him.

PEOPLE LIKE THAT

For the secret power of lawlessness is already at work;
but the one who now holds it back will continue to do so
till he is taken out of the way.

2 Thessalonians 2:7

Our culture may say people like you and me—Christians—are the problem with this world. But God actually restrains evil through believers.

Christians have acted throughout history as promoters of human rights. It was Christians in the Roman Empire who worked to ban infanticide, gladiatorial combats, and other cruelties. Christians outlawed human sacrifices and were the moral force behind the abolition of slavery, first in Europe in the Middle Ages and then against the later slave trade. Many of our laws that defend human rights come from our Christian heritage.

SWEET FREEDOM IN *Action*

Today, speak up unintimidated to remind others and yourself that God always uses Christians to affect the culture in large ways and small, and prepare yourself for His plan to use you. Refuse to be marginalized.

HE'S THE OVERCOMER, I'M NOT

...for everyone born of God overcomes the world. This is the victory that has overcome the world, even our faith. Who is it that overcomes the world? Only the one who believes that Jesus is the Son of God.
1 John 5:4–5

We'll never actually overcome the world, but having a relationship with God allows us to survive it as He does the overcoming.

When writing this page, I think of my youngest son's babysitter. Karen is a saint. It's been a heck of a season for me, but much more so for Karen, whose husband is fighting pancreatic cancer as I write this. When I read this verse, I think of those who experience real hardships, real tragedy, and I'm in awe of their resilience. Our Savior is the ultimate overcomer. Karen and I have concluded that relying on Him is the only way we can survive this world and its hardships. He does the overcoming for us.

As much as I rely on self-discipline and dogged determination to accomplish a task or to get through another trial, I find that having faith in God and turning to Him with hope is really the only way to deal with life.

Karen and I are united in the hope of Christ. I hope you are too.

SWEET FREEDOM IN *Action*

Today, reflect on how you handle your serious struggles in life. Who—or what—do you turn to for guidance and support? If it's not God, then you need to remind yourself of this passage of Scripture, and of He who overcomes the world.

WOLVES IN SHEEP'S CLOTHING—I'VE MET THEM, AND SO HAVE YOU
*Watch out for false prophets. They come to you in sheep's
clothing, but inwardly they are ferocious wolves.*
Matthew 7:15

Alaska has its wolves. You can't miss them. They're ferocious and deadly. But at least they're obvious.

Washington, D.C., has wolves, too, though they dress in sheep's clothing—at least at election time.

Still, if you watch long enough, and closely enough, you'll catch them stripping off their disguising, flea-ridden wool and exposing their wolfish fangs.

The media obviously push certain politicians to the forefront, and more often than not it's the most liberal of the bunch. In other words, they're pushing false prophets who want to sell you a bill of goods while they "fundamentally transform" our country.

So do your own homework on candidates and issues, and investigate what's beneath the sheep's clothing. The voting record—and business record—of a politician will tell you a lot of what you need to know.

We have a responsibility to elect leaders who will bear good fruit. That means we need to be wise in the voting booth. It means that if you vote for a liberal Democrat, don't be surprised if he appoints an activist judge who overturns the will of the people, or if he hires left-leaning bureaucrats who regulate you out of basic constitutional rights. (And by the way, keep an eye on Republicans too: most of them need to get serious about out-of-control spending.) When you vote for politicians, think about the fullness of what they can do, how they will make decisions, how they will vote or lead. It's a heavy responsibility—but it's ours.

SWEET FREEDOM IN *Action*

Before any election, don't listen to the mainstream media insisting you vote for their chosen one. Look out for false prophets, for wolves in sheep's clothing. Inform yourself and make your decision—and remember that you are morally accountable for your vote.

HANDS OFF

The wicked lie in wait for the righteous,
intent on putting them to death...
Psalm 37:32

Some people joke that stalking is when two people go for a long romantic walk together but only one of them knows about it. That's a funny line, but stalking is not a funny subject. Some families go through hell on earth because of the unwanted, threatening attention of stalkers.

I know this personally because my family has been stalked, and I've had to face some unsettling situations.

Stalking is a serious criminal issue, and one where the faith community can help by reassuring our fellow citizens that it's okay to arm yourself for protection, that it's okay for men to accept their traditional role as family protectors, and that our culture and media need to clean up their acts—especially their obsession with celebrity and sex.

Christians, of all people, should know that original sin is real, that evil is real, and that we need to protect ourselves against it, both spiritually and physically; none of us should passively become a victim.

Today's Scripture reminds us that it's not paranoia for us to believe that evil lies in wait for us. All too often it does, as local news reports and crime reports attest. Obviously there are wicked people out there. Be ready to stop them.

SWEET FREEDOM IN *Action*

Today, remember that you have a God-given right to self-defense. Be prepared to exercise it.

HONOR THE CREATOR BY TAKING CARE OF THE CREATION
Therefore honor God with your bodies.
1 Corinthians 6:20

D id you know scientists have discovered a food that actually reduces a woman's drive to exercise by 90 percent?

Her wedding cake.

Hey, it doesn't do wonders for men either.

That's a joke, but behind it is the truth that a lot of people give up their dedication to fitness after they get married. But that's unfair to your spouse— you should both want to be healthy for each other. It's also unfair to your children. You need to set a good example, and they need you to be healthy.

A lot of people are adopting a simple, non-faddish, back-to-nature "caveman" diet—or, as I see it, eating what God created us to eat; I think of Adam and Eve eating paleo.

Personally, I try to adhere to a low-carbohydrate, ketonic way of life—as often as possible eating foods we harvest ourselves. High protein, good fats, low processed carbs—this lets a body turn the organic protein (that we usually have to hunt or catch first!) and natural fats into consistent and reliable energy. This way you avoid blood-sugar spikes and energy dips caused by the processed, high-carb, "low-fat" foods of the standard American diet ("SAD"). I'm not a doctor or a dictator so I would never tell you what to eat. I can only tell you what works for me, many other people, and I do believe Adam and Eve. And this way of life leaves room for the occasional homemade cinnabun!

SWEET FREEDOM IN *Action*

It honors our Creator to take care of His creation. Today, adopt some healthy habits as a courtesy to those you love and the God who loves you.

MY FAVORITE MOTORHEAD

Through the victories you gave, his glory is great;
you have bestowed on him splendor and majesty.
Psalm 21:5

I adore hardworking mechanics and motorheads, those who can fix anything and love the roar of a combustion engine because they know it'll get us where we need to go. My favorite one of all is the iconic off-road racer, Walker Evans, whom I mentioned earlier.

Nicknamed "The Legend," my buddy's one of the best race car and truck drivers ever.

He was inducted into the Off-Road Motorsports Hall of Fame in 2004 and into the Motorsports Hall of Fame America in 2015. I got the chance to attend the latter ceremony in Detroit. He's won 142 victories and 21 championship titles in short course and desert racing events during his career, and it was an honor to see someone receive the accolades he deserves. To think, he first raced in a Rambler sedan, which is the first car I remember riding in as a little girl—we would pack into my dad's light blue Rambler on family road trips along Alaska's one and only main highway.

Besides my dad, Walker lives life more vibrantly than anyone I know. He's one of my heroes…and definitely my favorite Californian. Over the years, we've hunted, fished, raced cars, and snowmachined together—there's something so energizing about being around people who are full of life and fun. They say you become the average of the people you surround yourself with, and Walker ups my average.

When Jesus said He came to give us life—and then added that we'd have it "more abundantly"—that message feels extravagant. The fact that God cares about the quality of our day-to-day existence and our energy level and our enjoyment in life is pretty mind-boggling.

SWEET FREEDOM IN *Action*

Today, surround yourself with people who—like Walker—give life instead of suck it from you. In addition, try to become someone dedicated to the fullness of life so you can share vibrant living with others.

A GIFT TO THE EMBARRASSED
My Father, who has given them to me, is greater than all;
no one can snatch them out of my Father's hand.
John 10:29

A day after I called out the media for publicly exploiting young victims in an embarrassing, gossip-ridden teen sexual-abuse case, not excluding in my criticism a host who happened to work for my employer, I received pretty startling news.

I'd gotten canned by Fox.

At least I think I got canned. I've to this day never actually been told, "You're outta there," but my bosses left a message with my husband to make sure I knew they wouldn't be renewing my contract. So, after years of working with a good television team, always on good terms, it abruptly ended. Eh, sometimes you win, sometimes you learn. That's the media business.

The official report was that the network and I had agreed to part amicably; reporters, of course, gleefully announced that I'd been fired.

The fact is, I was happy Fox had given me the opportunity; Fox was perfectly within its rights not to renew my contract for any reason at all; and I certainly wasn't going to complain about it because I respect the network and its right to do what it's got to do.

I've been on both sides of an "axing." It can be awkward to have to fire someone; it can be embarrassing to be fired.

Your natural instinct is to hide. But, really, there is no place to hide.

The first recorded incident of embarrassment is when Adam ate the apple and then tried to hide. That didn't fool God one iota. In the end, only God's opinion matters. Do right by Him.

SWEET FREEDOM IN *Action*

Read Genesis again, and rest assured you don't need to hide; there's nothing you can hide from God anyway. Trust in His mercy and judgment.

CIVIL DISOBEDIENCE: YOU IN?
Peter and the other apostles replied:
"We must obey God rather than human beings!"
Acts 5:29

The English historian Lord Acton wrote, "Power tends to corrupt and absolute power corrupts absolutely. Great men are almost always bad men, even when they exercise influence and not authority: still more when you superadd the tendency or the certainty of corruption by authority."

People can't seem to help themselves. When they get a taste of power, they often abuse it and lord it over everyone else. That includes legislators, chief executives, and even judges (and justices of the Supreme Court). Laws, made under the guise of authority, are sometimes *bad* laws that oppress the innocent.

If a law is unjust and opposed to God's laws, we need to oppose it. Throughout our history—most famously with the abolitionist movement—Americans have done just that. Like the apostles, we must obey God's eternal moral law rather than the human-made law of the moment.

Our Founding Fathers were suspicious of government power—especially the power of the federal government—because they too understood that power corrupts. We should always view government power suspiciously and reject it when it oversteps its bounds.

SWEET FREEDOM IN *Action*

Today, pledge to support candidates for office who actually believe in limited government as set forth in our Constitution and who give paramountcy to God's eternal law.

AMERICAN EXCEPTIONALISM
In his name the nations will put their hope.
Matthew 12:21

O ur exceptional nation, so vibrant with ideas and passionate debate, is a light to the rest of the world. Some people believe the phrase "American exceptionalism" sounds boastful, but it's not about being better than other nations.

It is about standing firm on our foundational principles that all men are created equal and that their fundamental rights come from God not man. These principles have freed millions, not only in our own country, but around the world. American exceptionalism liberated Europe from the Nazis, saved parts of the world from atheist communism, and is working today to stop the Islamic State and other radical extremists from their reign of terror.

It's impossible to stomach the lies coming from abroad, and even from within our own borders, that say we should be anything less than proud of what America stands for. President Andrew Jackson said, "Americans are not perfect people, but we are called to a perfect mission."

SWEET FREEDOM IN *Action*

Today, celebrate the things that make this the greatest nation in the world! We don't need a "fundamental transformation" of America; instead, we need a restoration of all that is good and strong and free in America!

TIME FOR MORE TEA

He does not keep the wicked alive
but gives the afflicted their rights.
Job 36:6

We the people. That's what so many Americans have rallied around since the unstoppable Tea Party grassroots movement emerged. It resonates deeply with our Founders' vision for an America created by the people and for the people, while it fights to ensure our lives are not ruled by the elites in Washington.

And where do these convictions originate? We believe we're created in God's image and thus have God-given rights that we must protect from the destructive forces of the federal government.

Even as the liberal media mock our ideals and our leaders, and even dare to mock our God, we have continued to stand for what is right. We stand because our hope comes from above, not from our TV screens and from Washington. Liberal elites put patriots down and mock them because they're scared of conscientious, independent citizens. They look around and realize there are more of us than there are of them. They're scared, because they see how people flock to a message of truth and hope. Patriots will keep winning because when the true biblical hope that the Founders enshrined in our Constitution is held up next to the façade of hope that this world offers, hope rooted in Christ *always wins*.

SWEET FREEDOM IN *Action*

Today, support those in your community who are truly fighting to up-hold our one nation under God! Get involved in a local campaign for a candidate who stands for these principles.

DOG EAT DOG

Finally, all of you, be like-minded, be sympathetic,
love one another, be compassionate and humble.

1 Peter 3:8

We live in a dog-eat-dog world, where people feel the need to get ahead by any means necessary. When we tell our competition to "break a leg," we might actually mean it. When our opponent says, "Bite me," we just might. Think Nancy Kerrigan and Tonya Harding. Or, more literally, Evander Holyfield and Mike Tyson. You get the idea.

The antithesis of this "me first" spirit can be found in charitable organizations that help those in need. In 2009, this spirit was present when five women from Texas read a book by their fellow Texan Marcus Luttrell. After reading the bestselling book *Lone Survivor*, they felt they should do something to give back to soldiers and their families. They created a nonprofit organization called the Boot Campaign and got celebrities like Dwayne Johnson, Garth Brooks, Dolly Parton, and the cast of *Sons of Anarchy* to be photographed wearing combat boots.

Their motto? *Walk a mile in their shoes.* The organization—whose goal is to "awaken the patriot in all of us"—now gives more than $2 million to the military community each year. I wear their dog tag–inspired necklace on TV and love it when it's recognized. The group's selflessness is an inspiration.

SWEET FREEDOM IN *Action*

Today, perform an act of charity for someone in your family or your community. Be the inspiration.

THE GOSPEL AND RACIAL RECONCILIATION

*For there is no difference between Jew and Gentile—the same
Lord is Lord of all and richly blesses all who call on him, for,
"Everyone who calls on the name of the Lord will be saved."*
Romans 10:12–13

One of the great things about Christianity is that it reminds us that
everyone—rich or poor, black or white—is created in God's image.
We are all children of God.

As an American, I am proud of the great racial progress our country
has made in ensuring equal rights for all, regardless of race.

But I have to tell you—I'm appalled by the way liberals still try to divide
this country. They deny that ethnic minorities can be conservative—and
in fact shamelessly attack everyone from Clarence Thomas to Michelle
Malkin on ethnic grounds just because they're conservative. It's shameful
the way some liberals exploit issues involving law enforcement to pit some
communities against the police.

Our country can be united. Our faith can help us live out the truth
that we are all created in God's image. Let us do so and give all the glory
to God.

SWEET FREEDOM IN *Action*

Today, remember that every believer is an equal heir to the kingdom of
God, and think about ways you can spread this biblical truth throughout the land.

You Are an "Heir of Freedom"
I will walk about in freedom, for I have sought out your precepts.
Psalm 119:45

As Americans, we have been given a great gift of freedom, and God's Word makes clear that He expects us to steward our gift well.

Our Founders understood this responsibility. Out of service to their fellow Americans, thousands of men now long-forgotten charged the cannons, ran into bayonets, suffered in the trenches, and gave their lives so that we could live freely. We can't squander what they gave us or what the next generation expects from us.

President Ronald Reagan said: "Freedom is never more than one generation away from extinction. We didn't pass it to our children in the bloodstream. It must be fought for, protected, and handed on for them to do the same, or one day we will spend our sunset years telling our children and our children's children what it was once like in the United States where men were free."

Our Founders called us the "heirs of freedom," and as such we have a duty to those who have already paid the price for us to live in freedom, and we have a duty to those who will come after us.

Sweet Freedom in *Action*

How is God calling you to fight for freedom today? Do you need to register to vote? Do you need to volunteer in a local campaign for a freedom-loving candidate? Do you need to run for public office yourself? Ask God to show you how He wants to use you to protect this blood-bought gift.

WARS AND RUMORS OF WARS
In this world you will have trouble. But take heart!
I have overcome the world.
John 16:33

Televised images of war assault your senses, and personal battles assault your soul. Every aspect of life seems under fire. Our society now feels like it sits on shifting sand, almost unrecognizable from the country we grew up in. It's easy to give in to fear and depression.

Jesus warned us that we'd face persecution, tests, and trials. He also knew what we'd need to survive and thrive. Jesus said we should cling to the blessed assurance of His limitless love for us, His children, His followers. In tribulation, He tells us to be of good cheer anyway. If He says it, then I'm going to do it. I'm tired of the bad news; I choose to cling to the good news: He has overcome this world!

SWEET FREEDOM IN *Action*

Today, trust that God's love will give you authority over doubt and hopelessness. God is the same yesterday, today, and tomorrow. He's taken care of you in the past; He'll do it again.

HOLIER-THAN-THOU IS WHACK THEOLOGY
*You see that a person is considered righteous
by what they do and not by faith alone.*
James 2:24

"Wait a minute! That verse just contradicted 'justification is by faith alone'! I can't keep up, so I give up!" It's easy to go there with confusion over theology, so it's great to have charismatic, knowledgeable preachers with platforms who set us straight. Joseph Prince explained to his television audience what sweet freedom really is when explaining that we don't have to impress God to be justified. Anxiety-ridden people brought up in legalistic homes turn to rebellion. Living in anticipation of condemnation for imperfection, they're scared and dread-filled, knowing they'll never meet demands for mistake-free, totally sinless lives, or boy-oh-boy are they in trouble. That kind of existence is impossible. So, giving up, they tend to rebel.

Christianity accepts us as we are, flaws and all, so says Romans 4. That's not Joseph Prince's opinion—it's gospel.

He explained that James 2 isn't talking about justification before God, but of man. Since man is fallen, proving ourselves to each other is a different ballgame from justification in Christ. The Apostle Paul teaches us that God isn't impressed with man's works. Our efforts and accomplishments don't seal the deal and buy us a room in heaven.

This blows the earthly minds of people who've had holier-than-thou upbringings, people who have been fed guilt and condemnation because they've believed it's all about how "good 'n' holy" they are. Christianity is about faith—and forgiveness.

SWEET FREEDOM IN *Action*

Today, let's apologize for scaring anyone into miserably striving for impossible living. We turned Christianity into a "religion" instead of the grace-filled personal relationship with God that makes it a joy to try to do right by works. Salvation is according to His glory—through faith—thank God! Ephesians 2:8 says salvation is a free *gift*. It's not earned or deserved by striving through exhausting efforts to impress Jesus. Relax! Just take a breath! No guilt! Keep It Simple, Sweetheart!

CHRISTIANITY IS NOT A CHECKLIST

Come to me, all you who are weary and burdened, and I will
give you rest. Take my yoke upon you and learn from me, for
I am gentle and humble in heart, and you will find rest for
your souls. For my yoke is easy and my burden is light.
Matthew 11:28–30

*R*ead your Bible every day. Pray. Don't yell at the kids. Tithe 10 percent. No slang. No swag. No purple streaks in teens' hair. Do you ever feel suffocated by the things you need to do in order to be a "good person"?

The Pharisees loved to invent new rules and condemn people for not living up to their impossibly strict standards. In fact, they called their religion a yoke, which is a harness for restraining oxen and making them haul around heavy things. These holier-than-thou types bragged about their holiness, how many rules they followed, and how they made their yokes even heavier.

Then Jesus came and changed everything! He rescued those who had tried and failed to be "good people." He said it was impossible to accomplish enough to earn God's love; instead, we should focus on faith and accepting God's grace. God accepts us as we are. He's not sitting in heaven with a checklist, shaking His head at us and waiting for us to get it together. He only wants us to avoid sin and stay faithful.

SWEET FREEDOM IN *Action*

Today, don't get depressed or overwhelmed by the things you should be doing. Think of what Christ *has already done* and rest in Him.

First Responders Instructed to Pray

In my distress I called to the Lord; I cried to my God
for help. From his temple he heard my voice; my cry
came before him, into his ears.
Psalm 18:6

"Can I do anything to help?" We've offered this to more than one person going through a hard time.

"Only pray," he or she might respond.

If I'm honest, I'm always a little disappointed in that answer. There's a part of me that likes to go into action when bad things happen, when my friends or family are in trouble. Tangible actions make me feel like I'm actually helping…like I've stepped into the situation and moved the dial just a bit toward "better," and I can admit that "just" praying doesn't always seem sufficient.

Maybe this admits to a misunderstanding of the latent, untapped power of prayer.

Oswald Chambers said, "We tend to use prayer as a last resort, but God wants it to be our first line of defense. We pray when there's nothing else we can do, but God wants us to pray before we do anything at all."

Sweet Freedom in *Action*

Today, think of the people in your life who are struggling. Before you shut this book, decide to help them, but first and foremost, pray for them and accept the Holy Spirit's assurance in prayer's sufficiency.

BE A WATER WALKER
"Come," he said.
Matthew 14:29

This is an amazing account of a miracle, when the disciples of Jesus went out onto the water while Jesus was on a mountainside praying. Night fell, and the winds and waves buffeted the boat. I'm sure they were afraid.

Just before dawn, Jesus left the mountain and went out to the boat. He didn't swim. He walked. You may have heard this as a child in Sunday school, but try to hear it anew. He walked on water. Not frozen Lake Lucille outside my window, which allows you to walk on it easily half the year, we're talking a thawed surface—the *Sea of Galilee*!

"It's a ghost!" the disciples shrieked. Jesus identified Himself and tried to calm them.

"Take courage. Don't be afraid!"

"If it's you," Peter said, doubtfully, "tell me to come to you on the water." Okay, Jesus replied. "Come."

Peter's first steps were filled with awe and confidence as he kept his sights ahead—on Jesus. But then, analogous to many of our lives, Peter lost focus and looked down. He saw the storm. Overwhelmed by the sight of the waves and the wind, he began to sink. Taking his eyes off the prize, in his descent it was only Jesus, ever loving, ever forgiving, who could reach down and pull him to safety.

SWEET FREEDOM IN *Action*

Today, you'll face situations requiring big faith to step out. Walk to the prize by keeping your head up, focused on the Lord's outstretched hand to help you. Be a water walker.

SIN

If you do what is right, will you not be accepted? But if you do not do what is right, sin is crouching at your door; it desires to have you, but you must rule over it.

Genesis 4:7

S in.

Now, there's a word we don't hear much anymore. It became passé when doing things God's way became uncool—which was right around the time we started thinking we know better than He does. There was a time when it was a part of our culture to acknowledge faith publicly, pray, go to church, read the Bible as a family—and repent when we sinned.

Yes, "sinned."

It's common now to blame evil on everything but our selfish, free-will choices. Instead, we make excuses: it's due to addiction or drama from the past or some sort of instability. While these things definitely exist, sometimes sinning is just choosing to do things our own way. You want to get right with God? Then do things His way.

Sin exists, and God's justice demands a penalty for sin. That penalty, ultimately, is death. If that were the end of the story, it would be a sad story indeed. But the second part of our verse today brings good news! We don't have to succumb to sin or pay its price. Jesus already paid it. He offers eternal life to all who accept His free gift of forgiveness and salvation.

SWEET FREEDOM IN *Action*

Today, you'll have the opportunity to acknowledge that thing you do is not a "habit" or a "personality quirk" but *sin*. We're given strength enough to stop it when we accept God's free gift.

THE GOLD MINER'S NUGGET
Therefore do not worry about tomorrow,
for tomorrow will worry about itself.
Matthew 6:34

If my family and I are spotted on a flight, we're sometimes inundated with well-wishers, not-so-well-wishers, and the merely curious in the tight aisles, complicating life for peace-loving travelers. I feel bad about that, so I travel as inconspicuously as possible, but sometimes my annoying voice gives me away.

"More peanuts here in the back of the bus, eh?"

"You betcha!"

A grizzled old gold miner turned around. Recognition flashed across his face.

"You have a platform and a voice," he said, handing me a card. His hands were rugged, permanently etched with work ethic, adorned with a roughly hewed gold nugget ring. "People need encouragement to hang in there for the U.S. of A. Tell them this." He tapped the card.

It read:

There are two days in every week about which we shouldn't worry; two days kept free from fear and apprehension—Yesterday with its mistakes and cares, its faults and blunders, its aches and pains. It's passed, beyond our control. And Tomorrow—the sun will rise, either in splendor or behind a mask of clouds—it will rise, also beyond our control. This leaves only Today. Any man can fight the battles of just one day. It's when we add Yesterday's and Tomorrow's burdens that we break down. It's not the experience of Today that drives men mad—it's holding on to days you can't even control.

Thank you, Mr. Shell. That is gold. I'll tell them.

Sweet Freedom in Action

Today, take a deep breath and give up your control to God. It was His all along anyway.

LAST DAYS' LAWLESSNESS

*There will be terrible times in the last days. People will
be lovers of themselves, lovers of money, boastful, proud,
abusive, disobedient to their parents, ungrateful, unholy,
without love, unforgiving, slanderous, without self-control,
brutal, not lovers of the good, treacherous, rash, conceited,
lovers of pleasure rather than lovers of God....*

2 Timothy 3:1–4

It's certainly hard to argue we're not living in the last days as described in the Bible. Everything in these verses matches up with our current circumstances; there's a never-ending road of examples lately. Our culture, and Western civilization as a whole, has been declining for a long while—but things can look especially grim today. We do seem to live in evil times when evil is celebrated—whether it's in the brazen rejection of the Gospel or in the unashamed brutality of terrorist groups like ISIS.

A surprising number of our fellow Americans don't like the word "evil." They're always voicing the need for "tolerance" or "understanding"—or what you and I would call "moral relativism."

But these same people sure are keen on trying to legislate "evil" away when it comes to issues like guns, as if gun control laws (that only the good guys will follow) are a solution rather than an added problem.

The fact is, evil doesn't exist in guns or whatever else some of our lawmakers try to legislate away. It exists in the human heart. And the only cure for that, ultimately, is in God. But some people don't want to acknowledge that fact. They don't like "God talk," and they don't like to confront the reality that they have created a far less wholesome culture than we used to have.

We need to get that culture back.

Today, inevitably, you'll come across examples of sin running rampant, so when it hits you, pray for a cultural deliverance, and also take action. Support policies and a culture that encourage good behavior and discourage or punish the bad.

REAR END IN PEW

*...not giving up meeting together, as some are in the habit of
doing, but encouraging one another....*
Hebrews 10:25

Y ou'll let me be real in this devotional, right?
For years, it's been somewhat of a struggle to get it all together
on Sunday mornings to see our whole brood inside four walls of a conventional local church. For a variety of reasons, it's not been easy to get emotionally engaged or rooted in one church building this past decade while
on a public roller coaster ride, reasons including the haters who attack
churches we may attend—which is entirely unfair to the church. I'm not
using anything to excuse absences, because I do want my kids growing up
in Sunday school as my siblings and I did. I love church leaders and congregants who are in it for the right reasons.

Confession is good for the soul, and I know I need to try harder to get
plugged in to a good church body. Heaven forbid I get even closer to becoming a CEO—you know, a Christmas and Easter Only churchgoer.

The Apostle Paul says that being a Christian entails certain actions
that require other people. For example, he says to be baptized, to "eat
together at the Lord's table," and to stay connected to Jesus through the
church body. Kinda hard to do that at Starbucks.

SWEET FREEDOM IN *Action*

Today, vow to get your butt—and the butts of your family and friends—
back into the pews at church. I'll try too.

My Old Alaska Home

For we know that if the earthly tent we live in is destroyed,
we have a building from God, an eternal house in heaven,
not built by human hands.

2 Corinthians 5:1

Recently, Todd and I galloped over to the Kentucky Derby with our dear Alaskan friend John Hendrickson and his beautiful, interesting, inspiring, accomplished wife, Marylou Cornelius Vanderbilt Whitney.

Yes, that was me in the viewing box—one once used by Queen Elizabeth—the only one in the Bluegrass State watching the spectacularly iconic horserace without a hat. Where would I find a derby hat in Wasilla? I'd asked John. He assured me it was fine, that I could go rogue yet again and still be welcomed down south.

When the magnificent animals stepped onto the track for the parade of horses, the band began playing "My Old Kentucky Home." The 160,000 people in the stands sang along—including me. (Though I had to read the words.)

The song has a mournful tune, and I marveled at how emotional and heart-tugging the idea of "home" seemed to be for all of us there. I don't think it has to do with tobacco fields and horses (in the case of Kentucky), or moose and mountains (in the case of Alaska). It has to do with God planting in our hearts a desire for home.

Sweet Freedom in *Action*

Today, remember that no matter how much you love your home and your life in it, the four walls that surround you now are just a shadow of what's to come.

STAND UP, STAND UP FOR (ULTIMATELY) JESUS
Speak up for those who cannot speak for themselves,
for the rights of all who are destitute.
Proverbs 31:8

Fifty years ago, twenty-eight-year-old Kitty Genovese was sexually assaulted and stabbed to death just steps away from her Queens apartment at three o'clock in the morning. The first sentence of a *New York Times* article described her murder: "For more than half an hour 38 respectable, law-abiding citizens in Queens watched a killer stalk and stab a woman in three separate attacks in Kew Gardens." During the thirty-five-minute attack, no one called the police except one neighbor…after Genovese was already dead.

Psychologists coined "the Genovese Syndrome" to describe the phenomenon of people refusing help to a victim if other people are nearby.

Fear can stop us from standing up for our fellow man, but it's no excuse. I worry that the Genovese Syndrome is getting worse as our culture teaches us not to take action ourselves, but to alert authority figures. Yes, we should call the police if we see a crime in action—but we also have a personal obligation to defend the defenseless.

Edmund Burke said, "When bad men combine, the good must associate."

SWEET FREEDOM IN *Action*

Today, ask God to give you courage and compassion. Look for examples of people who need defense and an ally; rise boldly to meet the challenge and save a civilized future!

"SMOLDERING STUBS" AND OTHER INSULTS
Do not lose heart because of these two smoldering stubs of firewood...
Isaiah 7:4

In my family, we love sports and we do play games.

I often quote Plato: "You learn more about someone in an hour of play than a year of conversation." That's why we invite people—including reporters and politicians, celebrities, potential business partners, and future in-laws, etc.—to join us out fishing, camping, snowmachining, building hunting camps, and playing our own Eskimo Bingo to get to know them better. Sports and play are where guards are dropped and true character gets revealed.

One thing, though—there is some trash talk. If you trash-talk and win, then you look confident. But if you're mouthing off and lose...well, at least you had the fun of mouthing off.

I have to assume that the verse in Philippians 2:3 (which says "Do nothing out of selfish ambition or vain conceit. Rather, in humility value others above yourselves....") simply can't apply to playing "H-O-R-S-E" in the driveway. Instead, I believe God Himself participated in a little trash talk in Isaiah to calm the worried King Ahaz of Judah about his northern rivals when He called them just "smoldering stubs." I like it that God used Isaiah to throw down some trash—and, in appropriate circumstances, I'm sure He doesn't mind if we do either.

SWEET FREEDOM IN *Action*

Today, pull out the Scrabble board and try to work "smoldering stubs" into your conversation. It might throw your opponents off their game, give them a snippet of Scripture they might not know, and remind us that God has a sense of humor.

THE PLANS OF THE DILIGENT

The plans of the diligent lead to profit
as surely as haste leads to poverty.
Proverbs 21:5

In 2014, Eritrean-born American Meb Keflezighi won the Boston Marathon. As a former refugee from East Africa, his journey is nothing short of inspirational and his victory was very emotional to those who knew his story. In addition to winning in Boston, Keflezighi won the New York City Marathon and an Olympic medal. He's the only one in history to do all three.

In his commencement address at National University, the patriotic, Christian man compared running to the real world. "Falling down is part of sports and life, but injuries heal and challenging circumstances can be overcome."

To see someone from a poor, war-torn country achieve so much should encourage us all to try our best. Like me, you probably don't have an Olympic medal in your future, but we can still start plugging away. Meb can be our inspiration as we seek to emulate the spiritual diligence of a long-distance runner.

SWEET FREEDOM IN *Action*

Today, grab an item on your to-do list, and have the stamina to cross the finish line and then run on to the next item. It's truly exhilarating!

LESSONS FROM ABE
So if the Son sets you free, you will be free indeed.
John 8:36

W hat a long journey from a humble log cabin to the White House. The road Abe Lincoln traveled had hardships—from the loss of family as a boy to the turmoil of a war-torn nation as a man. Without question, his faith and perseverance contributed to his Gettysburg Address, in which he asked that we be

> dedicated to the great task remaining before us—that from these honored dead we take increased devotion to that cause for which they gave the last full measure of devotion—that we here highly resolve that these dead shall not have died in vain—that this nation, under God, shall have a new birth of freedom—and that government of the people, by the people, for the people, shall not perish from the earth.

All these years later, it is imperative we make the same commitment!

SWEET FREEDOM IN *Action*

Today, ask God for the courage and will to fight for America's future in honor of those who did fight—and even died—for this country. Do something tangible for those who serve, and promise them that their sacrifices have not been, and will not be, in vain.

JOURNEY VS. DESTINATION

And God said, "I will be with you. And this will be the sign to you that it is I who have sent you: When you have brought the people out of Egypt, you will worship God on this mountain."
Exodus 3:12

Aerosmith's song "Amazing" emphasizes that life is about the "journey," not just arriving at the "destination." Who knew that song held such good theology?

When God led the children of Israel out of Egypt into the desert, He wanted them to find Him.

Relationship was the goal. Yes, He wants us to come into our "inheritance," but the "inheritance" that He had in mind was that of Abraham, Isaac, and Jacob—three men of God who knew Him, and walked with Him. His inheritance to them was that He promised to draw a people unto Himself.

That was the purpose of the journey of Exodus—to prepare God's people for freedom and a relationship with Him. The destination was not just the "promised land," but knowing God.

Similarly our life is not an end in itself—it is a journey of faith and preparation. It's all about the journey.

SWEET FREEDOM IN *Action*

Today, reflect on your own journey—are you traveling a true course toward your objective? If not, readjust where necessary, and then let's roll!

THE TRUTH ABOUT LOVE: IT'S MESSY

One who has unreliable friends soon comes to ruin,
but there is a friend who sticks closer than a brother.
Proverbs 18:24

We don't typically associate love with a command. We tend to see it as a feeling, which explains why when feelings fluctuate—as they do—we can easily check out of relationships that once had meant the world to us. We say we "just don't love them anymore." And it's true; we don't *feel* that we love them anymore, but that's because we've disobeyed the Lord's *commandment* to love one another.

Today's commitments seem so easily broken. So many marriages end in divorce; an incalculable number of people "uncouple" with their former friends.

But as Christians we should *choose* to love. We should *choose* to hang in there when times are rough. We should *choose* to believe the best in one another. We should *choose* to sacrifice for our family and friends.

One of the greatest gifts God has given us is friendship. I have been blessed with a loyal circle of sisters and lifelong girlfriends. We've gone through life's ups and downs, including births and deaths, marriages and splits, and now we experience our children's ups and downs, too...all together. Even when life gets turned inside out, we're there for each other. God intends that through friendship we might learn to love others the way He loves us. It's a tall order, but definitely worth the effort.

SWEET FREEDOM IN *Action*

Today, forgive friends and family for any imperfections. Remember, we're not all we're cracked up to be either.

THE WOUNDS OF A FRIEND

*Better is open rebuke than hidden love. Wounds from a friend
can be trusted, but an enemy multiplies kisses.*
Proverbs 27:5–6

Most people like to have loved ones tell us how wonderful we are and how rosy life is. If those are the only people we keep close, though, we don't grow. Friendships built on praise alone, those that only celebrate the good times, are not whole relationships. Some of the most important people in our lives are friends who'll say, "You're dead wrong," or warn, "She's no good for you," or even, "You've got a mint? No, not for me. For you." Those are the wounds to suck up because they come from people we trust.

This is not a popular message in today's culture where people get thrown for a loop after hearing some truth...not after our egos have been tickled all our lives. In my book *America by Heart* I called this out, dubbing this a "culture of undeserved self-esteem." Whatever you think of the show *American Idol*, it's at least a corrective, a real eye-opener for many, because suddenly people who've been told all their lives that they sing like Whitney Houston have to come face-to-face with reality. It's often not pretty and the judges can be harsh, but if a trusted friend had been truly honest along the way, the contestant might have found a better way to spend their time, money, effort, and resources. Honesty really is the best policy.

SWEET FREEDOM IN *Action*

Welcome real friendships into your life, and when someone you trust gives you a word of constructive criticism and correction, consider it and apply it. Equally important, love your friends enough to be honest with them as well.

IF IT SMELLS LIKE A SKUNK...
Do not be misled: "Bad company corrupts good character."
1 Corinthians 15:33

We overestimate our strength if we think that hanging out with nefarious characters won't affect us. That's like hanging around a skunk and expecting not to stink. I tend to believe we become the average of those with whom we are surrounded. Paul teaches the Corinthians to protect their character by being selective, because we're shaped by our buddies.

It's not just a matter of avoiding bad characters, of course, but of having friends who make us better. All of us need good examples in our own lives. We need friends who will encourage us to pick up our game when we're lagging, to set higher standards when we're being too easy on ourselves, to sometimes take us to Bible study when we'd rather lounge on the sofa, and to tell us when we're wrong.

Often, you can tell a lot about a person by their friends. It's important to have friends that make you better and don't try to lead you astray. It's like we tell our kids, "Show me your friends, I'll show you your future."

SWEET FREEDOM IN *Action*

Today, take inventory of your friends, pray for those who might not be walking the right path, and vow to spend more time with those who help you become a better person.

LAY YOUR BURDENS DOWN
Cast your cares on the Lord and he will sustain you;
he will never let the righteous be shaken.
Psalm 55:22

We've all had sleepless nights worrying about what the next day will bring. Will our country be safe? Will our kids grow up to know God? Will I be a good enough wife, mom, daughter, friend, governor, candidate, patriot? Will the cultural trajectory of this world turn around?

These worries are legitimate, but worry is just practicing doubt.

I treasure the moments my kids come home, curl up by me, and tell me about their hard days or what they're concerned about. What a joy it is as a mother to have your children ask for your advice and assistance.

This is what our Heavenly Father desires of us. His Word says He's delighted when we come to Him with our worries and problems. It should be comforting to imagine God putting His big arm around your shoulder, inviting you to share what's weighing you down. As much as we appreciate our relationships with family and friends, we—I, anyway—really have no one with the capacity to calm fears and point us perfectly in the right direction. Why not take Him up on the offer to lean on Him? He's "the One" with the power over our worries in the first place.

SWEET FREEDOM IN *Action*

Today, when you pray, put yourself in God's arms, curl up, and let go.

THE STRONG, DIGNIFIED WILDERNESS WOMAN

She is clothed with strength and dignity;
she can laugh at the days to come.
Proverbs 31:25

Some people think the Proverbs 31 woman is a meek, quiet, submissive little thing. Yet this verse speaks of strength, dignity, and hard work! A passive, silent woman is not what God has in mind.

And, boy, am I glad!

My Alaskan women friends are amazing examples of the gal in this passage. Women here hunt, fish, chop wood, plow snow, fix four-wheelers, set up camp, and play sweaty, messy sports. Women and men seem so equal in the Last Frontier! And real men aren't threatened by strong women.

Secular culture tells us that we need to be more like men in order to be successful, still claiming "it's a man's world." Segments of Christian culture tell us we need to be quiet and passive to be righteous.

Yet, when Solomon wrote about the ideal woman in Proverbs 31, he described a woman who was 100 percent feminine and 100 percent strong and dynamic at the same time. So it's not impossible! We should strive to raise girls to know they can be both!

SWEET FREEDOM IN *Action*

Today, male and female readers should contemplate Proverbs 31 in its entirety. Make a list of the attributes Solomon celebrates. Ask God to help us be the strong and dignified person He's created us to be.

A SIMPLE REMINDER ABOUT GOD
All your words are true; all your righteous laws are eternal.
Psalm 119:160

One Easter, our family hunted for eggs in many feet of new snow. Thankfully, brightly colored eggs are simple to spot. That weekend, I remember hearing Pope Benedict sum up the lessons of the Gospel in a simple yet profound way: "Life is stronger than death. Good is stronger than evil. Love is stronger than hate. Truth is stronger than lies."

In a world where truth seems passé and unimpressive, it's good to remember this straightforward, stabilizing truth.

It doesn't matter what the culture says, God's Word endures forever.

It doesn't matter what the Supreme Court says, God's Word is true.

It doesn't matter what the media say, God's Word is life-giving.

It doesn't matter what a blog post says, God's Word is kind.

It doesn't matter what a pop psycho-blah-blah says, God's Word holds the secret to peace.

It doesn't matter what social media commenters type, God's Word is joy.

SWEET FREEDOM IN *Action*

Today, ask God to remove the cultural haze. Press in to see clearly what He wants you to spot. Commit from this day forward to reject any word that is not of God.

DOGS ARE EASILY AMUSED. ME TOO.
I do not understand what I do. For what I want to do
I do not do, but what I hate I do.
Romans 7:15

Ever find yourself watching a dog chase its tail, thinking, "Dogs sure are easily amused." Then you realize—you're watching a dog chase its tail.

How often do we do this in our spiritual lives? We point out the sin in other people's lives while feeling self-righteous about ourselves. We gossip about our friends and mock our own goofy family members. My family has been the center of tabloid gossip and mockery for quite a few years now. I wish people paid more attention to their own wagging tails instead of spending time reporting on our lives—or worse, just making things up!

But this speaks to a deeper spiritual problem. Like Paul says in his letter to the Roman church, we often know the right thing to do and yet we choose to do the wrong thing instead. We want to be disciplined and work hard and stay focused, but we find ourselves wasting time on inconsequential things, or even on things that offend our Heavenly Father and hurt our fellow man. We must continually ask God to search our heart and protect us from the distractions of the enemy.

SWEET FREEDOM IN *Action*

Today, vow to fill your day with God-honoring activities. Choose to not waste time—accomplish that by focusing on His will. Sending up a prayer is never wasted time.

ENEMIES CAN'T GUM YOU TO DEATH

But I tell you, love your enemies and pray for those
who persecute you.
Matthew 5:44

Round-the-clock news coverage, nonstop social media, and a hyper-partisan press can make it feel like we're constantly battling an enemy. Demonizing opponents, spewing aggression, and manufacturing outrage and outright lies seem to come naturally to far too many people in politics, especially, I have to say, if they're on the left of the political spectrum. There are bad apples on both sides, of course, but folks on our side are far more likely to be wimps intimidated by the media while their side tends to do the intimidation.

So how do we respond?

Christ calls us to be like Him and love our enemies, and not to fear. As Paul reminds us in Romans, while we were still sinners against Him, Christ nonetheless died for us.

Christ died for our enemies too. Henry Wadsworth Longfellow built off of this truth with the important reminder, "If we could read the secret history of our enemies, we should find in each man's life sorrow and suffering enough to disarm all hostility."

You never know when a kind word or encouraging action will disarm an opponent. It allows you to see they're not so tough against you. When you're tempted to cower in fear of an opponent whose actions are truly devilish, remember Andrew Wommack's words: "The devil isn't a true lion; he just walks around roaring like one trying to intimidate the Body of Christ. But the truth is, he's had his teeth pulled, and all he can do now is gum you."

Today, think of someone—a boss, a neighbor, a family member—you find problematic and pray for them and yourself.

THE RUBY IN YOUR CROWN DEFERRED
To our God and Father be glory for ever and ever. Amen.
Philippians 4:20

This sure is a "me-centric" society. At every turn we're told to put our wants and needs and own happiness above everything and everybody else.

Jesus on earth was perfect proof that we're to live knowing there's much more to life than mere self. In fact, it's all quite the opposite of self! We were created for the sole purpose of bringing glory not to ourselves, but to God! And how great is that news? It counters a culture full of narcissism, which is vapid, empty, and ultimately unproductive.

It's awesome to know that when we put ourselves aside and focus on lifting up our fellow man and ultimately bringing glory to God, great things are achieved! The marble plaque on my kitchen counter reminds me of this. Engraved is President Reagan's quote: "It's amazing what can be accomplished when no one cares who gets the credit."

Our role in His story might mean we never get credit; we might plant seeds for others to harvest long after we're gone; but we know the effort we made, and so will God.

I also have a quote from Nelson Mandela stuck on my bulletin board: "As a leader, one must sometimes take actions...whose results will not be known for years to come. There are victories whose glory lies only in the fact that they are known to those who win them." Absolutely true.

SWEET FREEDOM IN *Action*

Today, forget about being recognized for your good works—in fact, make a point of giving and serving anonymously. That gives God the glory.

BIBLICAL WARRIORS "R" US!
Whatever you do, work at it with all your heart, as working for the Lord, not for human masters....
Colossians 3:23

I magine some alien visiting earth knowing nothing about Christians. He'd turn on the TV or catch a movie and maybe come away thinking Christians are one boring, judgmental, and mean earthly tribe.

Hollywood loves to depict believers as dull, dreary, and villainous.

But contrast this image with biblical characters, and a very different picture of what God intends for His people emerges. His characters are brave and bold! They're warriors! Wise and sharp and fit, they always led culture, not bending to it.

The trick is to be the person God meant us to be. He gave us all different talents and passions. There is no one model for Christian discipleship. As Dr. Martin Luther King Jr. said: "Set yourself earnestly to discover what you are made to do, then give yourself passionately to the doing of it."

SWEET FREEDOM IN *Action*

Today, realize that the best example you can give others of what it means to be a Christian is to look into yourself, recognize what your gifts are, and then develop them for the glory of God.

Sinking under Treasures

Watch out! Be on your guard against all kinds of greed;
life does not consist in an abundance of possessions.
Luke 12:15

One of the worst nautical disasters in British history was the 1859 wreck of the *Royal Charter* steam clipper. Hammered by hurricane winds and thrown upon the rocks, an estimated 450 people were killed. There were only thirty-nine survivors.

Among the passengers were gold miners who had struck it rich in Australia and were now returning to England. Many of them died weighed down by belts loaded with gold.

Their gold, far from ensuring their future, might actually have contributed to their deaths. Even worse, their greed likely prevented them from helping others. Not a single woman or child was saved from the ship.

Greed is a terrible thing, a corrupting thing, that can blind us to our real needs and certainly to the needs of others. If there is no truer love than laying down one's life for one's friends, how much truer is it that we should lay down belts of gold in order to save the lives of women and children?

Sweet Freedom in  *Action*

We should not put our trust in riches, but in our faith, which promises a brighter future than gold can ever deliver. Today, take stock of your possessions and take note of those things that might be dragging you down or distracting you from living a more abundant spiritual life. Remember that your real life jacket is your faith.

Discover the Awaiting Adventure

Do not conform to the pattern of this world, but be transformed by the renewing of your mind. Then you will be able to test and approve what God's will is—his good, pleasing and perfect will.

Romans 12:2

M ost everyone struggles at some point to find their purpose, but some suffer tremendously and needlessly in their search. They drift from job to job, relationship to relationship, always expecting their ship to come in—somewhere else. Nothing is good enough, unrealistic expectations are never met, and these desperate souls often blame others for their restless lot in life.

Conversely though, others settle on a single purpose that lets them get by, but is far below their potential. They spend their days plugging away to make enough money for a new toy or to buy the next big experience, but at the end of their day when the garage is full and the scrapbook is bursting, their heart is empty.

Life's highest purpose is found in the will of God. Your Designer did not just make a product, He wrote a story. To live out your unique story written by the Master Author is the most wonderful thing you can do. To find your storyline, transform your mind to know Him better.

God isn't writing a mystery, He's writing an adventure. Finding the story requires a new mindset—thinking less about self, more about Him and others.

Sweet Freedom in *Action*

Commit to a renewed mind this very moment. Shed old ways of thinking and discern the truth about God's storyline for you. Read about His character and ask Him to lead you into the fullness of a transformed mind, heart, and soul.

WEIGHTED WORDS

*But I tell you that everyone will have to give account on the
day of judgment for every empty word they have spoken.*
Matthew 12:36

It wasn't that many years ago that news traveled very, very slowly in the Alaskan territory. Perhaps a postmaster would tell a dog musher, who relayed the information on to someone in another village, who happened to operate on a broken shortwave radio connection. Even with the proliferation of the telephone, many places were off the grid. News of an event that happened far away in Washington might take weeks to arrive in the far reaches of America's largest state.

Enter the twenty-first century. Information flies lightning fast. It seems negative—and often incorrect—information travels the quickest. A good reputation that took decades to build can be destroyed with the press of a button, regardless of whether the accusation is true or false. Celebrity families learn about broken marriages via Twitter. A ball player is caught off guard when hearing his name as a pending trade. Parents of soldiers hear of attacks in real time and must process what that means for their sons and daughters at war.

More than ever, it is time to consider the power of words, because they often outrun intentions. The faster information travels, the more important it is that we get it right the first time. How would we speak if we really understood that our every word would one day be weighed for accuracy and intent—and by God our Almighty Father?

SWEET FREEDOM IN *Action*

Weigh your words today. Decide to speak life and truth with each one.

BE THERE

Give, and it will be given to you. A good measure, pressed down,
shaken together and running over, will be poured into your lap.
For with the measure you use, it will be measured to you.
Luke 6:38

In times of elevated stress, our ability to notice kindness increases exponentially. It's as if in moments when we're searching intently for any bit of normalcy or goodness, the smallest benevolence is more deeply appreciated.

Pregnancy is a season of joy, the celebration of a coming new life. Unfortunately, sometimes it's unexpectedly and shockingly cut short. Between my youngest daughters' births, I lost a baby at three months along. It was my second miscarriage. My dear doctor delivered the news with such tenderness that she cried with me. It wasn't an extended interaction, but it was deeply personal. Her compassion spoke volumes. It said, "I'm nowhere else but here with you. Let's work together." I will never forget how her kindness ministered to me in an otherwise lonely time of such grief.

Reflecting now, it makes me wonder what message I've sent to others in their times of stress—if a glance at my phone, a clipped sentence, or a head turned away made someone who was going through a hard time feel even worse. Oh, how I hope I've done something right: offered helpful words or a smile, or listened like a friend, anything that lightened their load like my doctor did for me.

SWEET FREEDOM IN *Action*

We all can listen more, smile more, offer a hand, and pour out genuine kindness to folks every day. We must *want* to be present with people more often. It makes a difference.

KEEP YOUR APPOINTMENTS

Therefore, as God's chosen people, holy and dearly loved,
clothe yourselves with compassion, kindness, humility,
gentleness and patience.
Colossians 3:12

Lots of believers stumble from day to day trying to hear God, wondering what His perfect will is for our lives, looking for it on bumper stickers or on a blog...or even in a daily devotion. Let me save you some wondering. God has preordained *good works* for you to do today. You will cross paths with someone who needs your help. You will connect with a person who needs encouragement. Your eyes will meet with a stranger's whose present situation seems insurmountable, and your brief smile will be the warmest part of his day. God has appointments with your name written on them—dates, times, opportunities for you to engage in acts of kindness that are an extension of His workmanship. He is everywhere, but He chooses to manifest Himself through the goodness of other people.

SWEET FREEDOM IN *Action*

What are we going to do today? The same thing we do every other day. Keep our appointments. Be aware of opportunities to do good for others. The kingdom is revealed when we act with loving kindness.

OPTIMISM DOESN'T HAVE TO BE CLICHÉ
Look to the Lord and his strength; seek his face always.
1 Chronicles 16:11

Former vice presidential candidate and American hero Admiral Jim Stockdale was a prisoner of war in North Vietnam. He was brutally tortured for eight years. "I never doubted not only that I would get out," he said, "but also that I would prevail in the end and turn the experience into the defining event of my life, which, in retrospect, I would not trade."

When asked why he survived while others didn't, he had a surprising answer. He said that others would pin their hopes on getting out by a certain date. "They were the ones who said, 'We're going to be out by Christmas.' And Christmas would come, and Christmas would go. Then they'd say, 'We're going to be out by Easter.' And Easter would come, and Easter would go. And then Thanksgiving, and then it would be Christmas again. And they died of a broken heart."

Pelagius noted this back around 400 AD, when he said, "There is no worse death than the end of hope."

No Christian should ever give up hope

SWEET FREEDOM IN *Action*

Today, don't fall for cultural pressure to be optimistic in a forced, obligatory way that is really more like a cliché. Instead, be realistic and prudent while trusting for the best.

Learn to Cope by Looking Away
Therefore, as we have opportunity, let us do good
to all people, especially to those who belong to the
family of believers.
Galatians 6:10

When a church called the Vineyard Community Church in Cincinnati moved from a small, cramped building into a massive new auditorium, there were lots of discussions—a few bordering on disagreement—about parking, kids' facilities, seating, etc. The one thing that was universally understood, however, was what would be emblazoned on the outside of the building, because it would be a unifying mission. Huge letters engraved into the structure read, "Small things done with great love will change the world." This phrase, often attributed to Mother Teresa, sums up the church's philosophy toward the community. A staff member's title, even, was "director of small things"! He was to find everyday opportunities for the church's thousands of attendees to reach out to others in kindness.

The benefits paid off. Many of those beneficiaries of their kindness were drawn into a relationship with God, because God's volunteers became missionaries of His grace.

In addition to the "small things" mantra was another phrase: "When we serve, we get a little better." Everyone comes to God with their own hurts and hang-ups, but in meeting others' needs, people take their eyes off their own problems and actually learn to cope in ways they never could if they only focused on themselves. There is an answer here to some of today's societal ills like boredom, lethargy, anxiety, substance abuse, and even disordered eating. Many problems come from focusing on oneself, a form of self-indulgence, instead of going out into the world to help others.

Sweet Freedom in *Action*

Kindness is a powerful force that works both ways. Step out of your comfort zone today in an intentional act of kindness. Guarantee you'll change a part of the world.

MY FASCINATION WITH FAITH
…I looked, and there before me was a door standing open in heaven. And the voice…said, "Come up here…"
Revelation 4:1

Knowing God is the highest purpose of the heart, and yet the most difficult. It reminds me of climbing Mount McKinley. You can't just wake up one morning and decide to climb the mountain; you train arduously for the feat. So it is with pursuing God; it's a lifelong, purposeful pursuit full of magnificent adventures, dangers, joys, peaks, valleys, and even encounters.

In Revelation 5, John sees the door open in heaven, someone sitting on a throne. He's immediately invited to "come up here." God wants to be known and visited!

We were all created with a spirit that longs to be fascinated, and to me this is a great part of being a Christian! When we find the pleasure of knowing God, nothing else compares, not even summiting that highest peak in North America. We can try to find fascination in money, relationships, busyness, but only by looking through that open door to see the glory of the One seated on the throne will our hearts finally be satisfied.

SWEET FREEDOM IN *Action*

Even when you feel exhausted and at the base of a mountain you have to climb, keep looking up to the Lord. He will sustain you. The door is open and is He saying, "Come on up!"

Damaging Doubt Gets Demolished

But when you ask, you must believe and not doubt,
because the one who doubts is like a wave of the sea,
blown and tossed by the wind.

James 1:6

D oubt is an inevitable part of life, and having some doubt—for instance, about politicians' campaign promises—can be a good thing. We don't want to fall for every sales pitch. We don't want to nod dumbly to the talking heads of the media. We don't want our votes or our money to be wasted on empty promises. As they say in Missouri, "Show me!"

But even more important than the mental check of doubt, we need trust. It is trust between people that builds bonds. It is trust that sustains a marriage. It is trust that allows a free society to function without everything being regulated and tied up in bureaucracy and red tape and a jungle of laws. Most important, it is trust in God the Father that sustains our faith.

Shakespeare said, "Our doubts are traitors, and make us lose the good we oft might win, by fearing to attempt."

Doubt can make our lives smaller. It can make us less courageous. It can keep us from taking the leaps of faith necessary to succeed. It can even keep us from listening to God.

Sweet Freedom in *Action*

Today, purge yourself of fear and doubt. Trust in God, pray for His Guidance, and abide by His Words.

WALKING IN SONSHINE

Whoever walks in integrity walks securely,
but whoever takes crooked paths will be found out.
Proverbs 10:9

"Walking in integrity." Is that more church talk that isn't applicable to the real world?

What exactly does that mean to a follower of Christ? We know we should live our lives so authentically that what we say lines up with our actions. We're created in God's image and likeness so it's in our DNA to want to be like Jesus, to represent Him well. We want to grow in faith and become better human beings, loving others as Jesus loves them. Every believer, though, messes up at some point. Most of us stray off the path more than once. When we're living an authentic life, we acknowledge our mistakes, ask God to forgive, move forward, and resolve not to mess up again.

When unbelievers see how we conduct ourselves, will we be perceived as hypocritical? That's the outcome if we speak like Christians but operate like the devil. Politically speaking it's like campaigning one way but governing another, which is enormously discouraging, albeit commonplace.

Walking in integrity is not optional, it's mandatory. We're called to be fishers of men, drawing people to Jesus. That mandate can only be carried out if we live authentic, transparent, Christ-centered lives. Honesty with ourselves and honesty with God will increase our effectiveness in leading others to Him.

SWEET FREEDOM IN *Action*

Today, be inspired to make sure that your Christian words inspire Christian deeds in yourself—and I'll do the same!

KEEP YOUR PROMISE

Do not be quick with your mouth, do not be hasty in your heart to utter anything before God. God is in heaven and you are on earth, so let your words be few.

Ecclesiastes 5:2

I've spent much of my life either participating in or commenting on politics, and there's one thing I've never gotten used to: politicians who make promises—dozens, even hundreds, of them—with either no intention or no real way of carrying them out. All they're really doing is trying to buy votes in the cheapest possible way, offering "solutions" that aren't solutions at all.

Our whole society has become cavalier about truth and keeping one's word. We've grown used to lies—from politicians especially, but others too. Because we've come to expect lies, we almost seem to have decided that lying is natural, like that old Clinton-era excuse, "Everyone lies about sex."

But not bearing false witness—not lying—is one of the Ten Commandments. That's how important it is. That's why we take oaths on a Bible. It's supposed to underline the importance of our being honest.

Our society would be a whole lot better off if we were all more honest. It would build trust, for one thing. It would also remind us just how careful we should be when taking a pledge or making a vow.

Promises should not be entered into lightly, because they're meant to be kept.

SWEET FREEDOM IN *Action*

Today, think twice before making a promise. If you have any outstanding obligations, meet them, and pony up. Let's not contribute to society's blasé attitude toward a promise.

THE UNGODLY SIDE OF THE FENCE

Refrain from anger and turn from wrath; do not fret—
it leads only to evil. For those who are evil will be destroyed,
but those who hope in the Lord will inherit the land.
Psalm 37:8–9

Ever look at your neighbor's yard and see that their grass is John Deere green while yours is grizzly bear brown? That they boast of cheating on taxes and their car is spanking new while your old beater has an inch of rust on it and petrified chicken nuggets *in* it? Have you wondered why that yahoo in the next cubicle over earns more money? And while he ignores the passed hat during office parties, he still nickel-and-dimes the business to death? Sometimes it seems that society rewards the unethical and doesn't much care about those who play by the rules.

But when we focus on those around us who prosper even though they aren't living right, it skews our perspective.

Here's the truth. Whatever you have—even if it's that threadbare quilt from your grandmother or a minivan held together with "Vote Anybody but a Liberal" bumper stickers—your life of virtue will be more profitable than living for yourself. God may allow people a temporary prosperity or triumph, but those devoted to following Him will get a heavenly reward. Trust God to deal with the jerk in the BMW who cut you off in traffic; your final inheritance will be a doozy.

SWEET FREEDOM IN *Action*

Today, be satisfied. God knows your heart and your actions. Keep them pure.

NO SAINTLY SHORTCUTS

May God Himself, the God of peace, sanctify you through and through. May your whole spirit, soul and body be kept blameless at the coming of our Lord Jesus Christ.
1 Thessalonians 5:23

When we repent of sins, we're justified by the Spirit and receive forgiveness. But we still live in mortal bodies in a fallen world, so we still fall short. Sanctification is a big word for something simple: becoming like Christ. Hopefully, we become more sanctified every day and can claim stronger faith than in our past. That's a good reason why us Sourdoughs shouldn't want to go back to our twenties for anything!

Though we're all in the process of being sanctified, we won't quite grasp it until we come face to face with Jesus Himself. Religious leaders peddle promises—*You, too, can be spiritually awesome if you just*…take your pick: have more Bible time, find an accountability partner, pray thirty minutes per day, tithe to this mission, buy that Christian book. But there's no shortcut to sanctification. It's the most basic thing and the most complicated thing you'll ever do. Die to self. Gain the world.

SWEET FREEDOM IN *Action*

Hang in there as He shapes and sanctifies you. There are no shortcuts.

GOOD NEWS IN EVERY EDITION!

*"The time has come," he said. "The kingdom of God
has come near. Repent and believe the good news!"*

Mark 1:15

L et's not forget what, exactly, the Gospel is. Here goes:
Our sin has separated us from God, but Jesus's death and resurrection can make things right between us. Our sins can be forgiven. This is good news, indeed! Especially for those of us keenly aware of our spiritual failings. (Don't get me started!) The Gospel is the same for me up here in Alaska as it is for a warm retiree in Florida. There isn't one Gospel for NASCAR fans, another for wine connoisseurs, another for hairstylists, and yet another for accountants. The Gospel is good news for Democrats and Republicans, for Lakers fans and Celtics fans.

The good news really IS good! Repent for your sins, believe in the Lord, and trust in God's goodness.

SWEET FREEDOM IN *Action*

Today, try to remember how good the "good news" really is. And remember that the Gospel is for everyone. The love and forgiveness of Christ knows no bounds.

PRAISE THE LORD AND PASS THE CHICKEN SOUP
Thanks be to God for his indescribable gift!
2 Corinthians 9:15

"Thank God!" we might whisper in relief when a situation turns for the better. "Praise the Lord!" is exclaimed after a thankful outcome. But praise isn't just for the good times; it's for every time. As they say in the marriage ceremony: "For richer, for poorer, in sickness and in health."

Thessalonians 5:18 teaches, "Give thanks in all circumstances; for this is God's will for you in Christ Jesus." That means when something doesn't go our way, we should still be grateful.

How can we do that? The key lies in our fundamental appreciation of the sovereignty of God. He is our Father and He's got the whole world in His hands. In other words, all will eventually be well—for nothing can keep us from our ultimate home in God.

SWEET FREEDOM IN *Action*

Today, demonstrate a thankful heart by appreciating everyone and everything around you. Utter a kind word, give a warm hug, and invite someone to share a meal tonight—and praise the Lord while passing the soup!

IN THE STORM BUT NOT OF THE STORM

*Jesus was in the stern, sleeping on a cushion. The disciples
woke him and said to him, "Teacher, don't you care if we
drown?" He got up, rebuked the wind and said to the waves,
"Quiet! Be still!" Then the wind died down and it was
completely calm.*
Mark 4:38–39

In the midst of a storm in our lives, we're very likely to panic. But we shouldn't, because we're not alone. God is always there with us, and He knows what to do.

A verse in Psalm 107 says, "He calms the storm, so that its waves are still. Then they are glad because they are quiet; so He guides them to their desired haven."

When visiting wives of deployed troops, and hearing of the logistical, practical, financial, and fear-laden hassles clouding their day, I try to encourage them with the words that can also help you in stormy situations: "When I'm in the storm, the storm is not in me."

That's the thing—there's no way we can avoid life's storms. But what we can control is our reaction to them—and the best way to do that is to put our trust in God.

SWEET FREEDOM IN *Action*

Today, remember that God is our salvation through every storm. He will see us safely into His heavenly port.

SELF-EXAMINATION: HEART HEALTH
*Let us examine our ways and test them, and let us
return to the Lord.*
Lamentations 3:40

I don't agree entirely with Socrates's claim that "the unexamined life is not worth living." My life doesn't get its worth through "Sarah-centric self-reflection." There's value, though, in periodic self-evaluation if we want a robust, healthy life.

Examine self and be warned: it's a little scary. Coming face-to-face with the realization that we have fallen short is sobering. Don't think that applies to you?

Luke 17:10 reminds us that even when we've done everything we're asked to do, we should really just consider ourselves unworthy servants. We haven't done anything exceptionally impressive in a surprise move to win God over, we've only done our duty.

But, the examination *is* liberating! We can drop the "holier than thou" pretense and just be normal. Not only does sin lurk in the world, imperfection and sin lurk within us, too. We need God's help in purifying our own hearts, in making course corrections. We need His grace. The Bible says He resists the proud but gives grace to the humble. Realizing our own shortcomings reminds us of how weak we really are in our own strength, and how reliant we are on God.

SWEET FREEDOM IN *Action*

Self-examination should always lead us to humble ourselves before God. Take time for that today.

SEE THE REAL PERSON
Stop judging by mere appearances, but instead judge correctly.
John 7:24

Do you get offended when filling out some endless bureaucratic form that asks you about "race"? It often seems that the people most obsessed with race, and with racial quotas for this, that, and everything, are the people who tell us we need to get over race.

But there's an easy way to get beyond race, and that's: don't judge by appearances. Don't judge a person on whether she is white, black, or Eskimo. Judge that person, if you're an employer, on skills; judge that person, if you're an educator, on academic achievement; judge that person, if you're a coach, on performance.

We aren't what we look like or what we do. We are children of God. That's true of every single one of us—no matter our color, our sex, or our sins.

SWEET FREEDOM IN *Action*

Today, as you go out in the world, look at everyone around you at the grocery store or driving around town or on a hike in the woods and remind yourself that every person you see is a child of God. Pray for them. And have your friends pray for you.

Qualify by Obeying Man's Law

Let everyone be subject to the governing authorities, for there is no authority except that which God has established. The authorities that exist have been established by God. Consequently, whoever rebels against the authority is rebelling against what God has instituted, and those who do so will bring judgment on themselves.

Romans 13:1–2

Driving my Tundra truck with its hardy V8 early one morning through Wasilla, no traffic in sight, I saw those flashing lights.

"You were driving sixty-three in a forty-five-miles-per-hour zone," the officer said.

I paid my fine and added, "But sir, l wasn't speeding. I was qualifying."

We are a nation ruled by law, not man. God is a God of law and order. Resisting sound authority is resisting Him, and consequences follow. My consequence for that early-morning sprint was $154 out of my pocket, but there are frequently tragic consequences to ignoring laws.

Beautiful, young Kate Steinle was murdered by an illegal immigrant who had already been deported five times. This seven-time felon purposely went to San Francisco, a "sanctuary city," knowing he wouldn't face consequences. An innocent woman was killed because those who were supposed to enforce laws and protect the public chose instead to ignore our immigration laws and put innocent people at risk. God expects just laws to be enforced. Those who break them must be judged accordingly.

Sweet Freedom in *Action*

Today, recognize that God is the author of all authority. Obey the law wholeheartedly—and make sure your political representatives do as well.

FORGIVING ALL

*"You intended to harm me, but God intended it for good
to accomplish what is now being done, the saving of many
lives. So then, don't be afraid. I will provide for you and your
children." And he reassured them and spoke kindly to them.*
Genesis 50:20–21

Many of us get caught up with petty grievances. We get angry when
kids march into the house with muddy boots. We lose our patience
with other drivers who don't know that the left lane is the FAST lane.

But we need to get a sense of perspective.

In the Old Testament, the patriarch Joseph endures hardship and
betrayal like we probably never will. His half brothers conspire against
him and sell him into slavery; they convince his father, Jacob, that he is
dead; and later, Joseph is falsely accused of rape and imprisoned.

Yet, he forgives those who harmed him and returns good deeds for
evil ones.

Reflect on his words: "You intended to harm me but God used it for
good; I forgive you and am happy to help."

That's forgiveness; *God's* kind of forgiveness; and it's the sort of forgiveness we're called upon to practice as well.

When we forgive others, we do as God would have us do, and we free
ourselves from those petty grievances that can ruin our day.

SWEET FREEDOM IN *Action*

Think about Joseph's patience, his willingness to forgive, his understanding that God can bring goodness out of any situation, no matter
how bad it seems at the time.

SOMETIMES A JOB CAN SEEM LIKE THE BOOK OF JOB
*If only my anguish could be weighed and all my misery
be placed on the scales!*
Job 6:2

When I was elected mayor, the mayor I'd defeated tried to have me recalled, and his cabinet refused to resign. I was stuck working with a truly disloyal bunch until I fired the ringleader, the police chief. (He sued me for that. I won.) It was hell for a couple of years.

I found myself, during that time, reflecting on the Book of Job. Job underwent trials far worse than mine; he endured, he remained faithful to God, he submitted to God's will, though he didn't immediately understand it, and in the end Job is vindicated.

The Book of Job was spiritual encouragement I needed at the time. It's a hard lesson but a good one.

The important thing to do, when you're in difficulties, is to stop asking God, "Why me?" You've been put in your circumstances for a reason. You might not understand the reason, but you need to remember that if you walk with God, you will triumph, because "God withholds no good thing from those who walk uprightly" (Ps. 84:11). For me, I went on to be reelected until I was term-limited out, serving successfully and moving up from there!

SWEET FREEDOM IN *Action*

It sounds like a cliché, but things really do happen for a reason. Don't try to figure out the reason—that's God's business. Just do the best you can, relying on God's grace and mercy.

LORD, DO YOU HEAR ME NOW?

Surely the arm of the Lord is not too short to save,
nor his ear too dull to hear.
Isaiah 59:1

Sometimes when we hit hard times we forget that God is absolute—all perfect, all powerful, and all attentive, including during our trials.

I know a good Christian man who was abandoned by his wife. In his grief, he doubted whether God heard his prayers—and he even came to wonder whether God existed at all.

If you haven't felt that way, ever, then you're a better believer than I am.

Seemingly unmerited suffering is one of the greatest challenges to faith.

What is the answer? Well, for me at least, the answer is not to stop praying, but to pray even harder. But one of the things we have to pray for is patience.

This is where trust comes in. In His time, He intervenes as He deems appropriate. It is not for us to try to guess the will of God. It is up to us to be faithful.

Walking with the Lord does not exempt us from trials. But in the depth of those trials, we need to remember that He cares. My friend did get through his dark hour and is a living reminder that life goes on and God blesses in unexpected ways.

SWEET FREEDOM IN *Action*

Today, remember to never doubt the long-term efficacy of prayers. Keep sending 'em up! Everything you say is heard in heaven, and God's mercy always comes shining through.

HOW TO PRAY

My God, I cry out by day, but you do not answer,
by night, but I find no rest.
Psalm 22:2

Our prayers—like David's—can be all over the place. We'll offer prayers of thanksgiving one day, prayers of self-pity (why me?) the next, turn around the following day with prayers of gratitude for our many blessings, then wail with prayers of despair that life is too hard, before offering prayers of complaint that God doesn't seem to be listening—or responding—at all. Good thing our wild fluctuations don't get God dizzy.

One reason for a "dry" or unsatisfactory prayer life is that we keep the focus on ourselves. That's a mistake, because our emotions, our circumstances, the good days and the bad days, can change every day.

But God is unchanging. He is constant. Instead of regarding Him as a genie at our ever-changing command, we need to think of ways to honor and serve Him. Our prayers are a way to seek out His will; that's why we pray that His will, not our will, be done.

SWEET FREEDOM IN *Action*

Today, reflect on whether your prayers are focused on giving glory to God.

SPIRITUAL WARFARE

*Then he continued, "Do not be afraid, Daniel. Since the first
day that you set your mind to gain understanding and to
humble yourself before your God, your words were heard,
and I have come in response to them."*
Daniel 10:12

Naturally, as humans, we focus on what we can see—and what we can see is sometimes depressing, whether it's the decline of our culture or the seemingly endless fight against Islamic terrorism. As these battles never seem won, it can seem as if all our prayers for America's spiritual health, or for peace, are for nothing.

The truth is, God hears our prayers, but the political battles we see are part of a far bigger war, a spiritual war that is constantly being waged between good and evil, God and the devil. We're only seeing shadowy glimpses of it; but what we do see can illuminate the fact that the battle takes time.

The Soviet Union existed for decades before it collapsed. Radical Islam has been a threat to Christianity for well over a thousand years. Our own domestic culture war will continue until America enjoys another Great Awakening.

The thing to remember is that through all these great struggles, prayer is ammunition. Even when we're sitting on our sofa at home, we can fight evil by praying. Prayer is a power that's in all our hands. So lock and load.

SWEET FREEDOM IN *Action*

Today, pledge yourself to be a prayer warrior—and never give up the fight!

Jesus Served, So What's Your Excuse?

For even the Son of Man did not come to be served, but to serve, and to give his life as a ransom for many.
Mark 10:45

King Jesus came to serve, not to be served. Many weren't expecting that sort of savior then. Many don't understand Him now.

It's too easy, given our fallen nature, for us to think that importance is measured not by service, but by a big salary, or by being famous, or by throwing our weight around.

Too many people worship celebrities, and too many celebrities seem to worship themselves, making outrageous personal demands and keeping a posse of hangers-on to make sure they're met.

Certainly in politics, so-called public servants seem to get the equation exactly backward. They think the taxpaying public should serve *them*.

Our Founding Fathers didn't think that. They had the equation right. They truly served their country in war and in peace.

And Jesus wants to follow His own example of service. Sure we can't raise the dead like He did, but if we're doctors we can cure the sick; through charity we can help the poor; and all of us can help make this a more Christian society by forgiving those who trespass against us.

Sweet Freedom in *Action*

Today, reflect on what service you can do for God—what special gifts He has given you and how can you share them.

LOVE YOUR FREEDOM? THANK A VET.

The greatest among you will be your servant.

Matthew 23:11

It's hard to top the service of America's veterans. I try to thank them nearly every chance I get.

Laying down your life for your fellow man—Jesus tells us that's the greatest love there is; it's the sacrificial love that He gave for us. Our veterans make sacrifices, sometimes with their lives, for our country.

With our all-volunteer military, every single man and woman in uniform has made a conscious choice to serve our nation—even if it means risking their own lives to protect us. They deserve our thanks, they deserve our prayers, and they deserve elected leaders in Washington who likewise put service above self and who work to keep America's military the best in the world.

When I was governor of Alaska, I was commander in chief of Alaska's National Guard, and I made it a priority to visit American troops wherever I could. In their far-flung posts, they are America's servant-ambassadors to the rest of the world; and they're the ones you can count on when things get tough. While so much of our society is losing its attachment to the ideals and virtues that have made our country the great nation that it is, the men and women in our armed services continue to embody these virtues and defend the freedoms we so easily take for granted.

SWEET FREEDOM IN *Action*

Today, remember that true greatness is measured in servanthood—and tell the vets you know how much you appreciate their service.

Make Mine a Double

Elisha then left his oxen and ran after Elijah. "Let me kiss my father and mother goodbye," he said, "and then I will come with you."…Then he set out to follow Elijah and became his servant.
1 Kings 19:20–21b

Okay, Elisha served Elijah…what's the big deal? The big deal is that Elisha came from a wealthy family and had a nice future all set out in front of him, yet he humbled himself and served Elijah.

But while he was content to follow Elijah, he burned with a wise ambition to serve God to the utmost. Instead of saying, "Oh, if I could just be *half* the man Elijah is," in 2 Kings 2:9 he asked for a *double* portion of Elijah's spirit—and his prayer was apparently answered, as he later performed *double* the number of miracles Elijah did. His final miracle occurred after his death, when a man's corpse was thrown into his tomb. As the decaying body touched Elisha's bones, the man was resurrected (2 Kings 13:21). Read it yourself! There's power in servanthood!

Elisha walked with Elijah, honored him, and learned from him as he served him. We're all called to a life of service. Our first tutor in serving others is, as it was with Elisha, the family. Next comes discerning God's call. God's preparing you for something—don't be afraid to serve an apprenticeship along the way.

Sweet Freedom in *Action*

You might have found your calling already, but there are plenty of young people out there who need to be shown the way. Today, help a young person in your life find his or her vocation, or support a group that helps develop young leaders.

WIN SOME, LEARN SOME

But blessed is the one who trusts in the Lord,
whose confidence is in him.
Jeremiah 17:7

Politics is like sports—there's a winner and a loser, and it's hard to be on the losing team. It's especially tough on young campaign staffers, and *particularly* on young *Christian* staffers. Their candidate was the *only* one who could get this country on the right track—couldn't God see that? Some even let political losses affect their faith.

There's a great Psalm that is particularly applicable: "Some trust in chariots and some in horses, but we trust in the name of the Lord our God" (Ps. 20:7).

Or to put into political terms: "Some trust in exit polls and some in voting booths, but we trust in the name of the Lord our God."

Everyone who works on political campaigns needs to commit to memory Psalm 146:3, "Do not put your trust in princes, in human beings, who cannot save." There's only one salvation—and that's in God.

Even when we win political victories, the victories are temporary. We enjoyed two terms of Ronald Reagan as president, but he was followed by a couple of less-than-stellar guys, one of whom dictated horrendously, in my humble opinion.

So while politics is important, remember what's even more important—our faith in God.

SWEET FREEDOM IN *Action*

Today, remember to keep the big picture in mind. Political victories come and go. But our lasting victory is the reward of faith.

Big Feet, Bigger Heart

*If anyone is poor among your fellow Israelites in any of
the towns of the land the Lord your God is giving you, do
not be hardhearted or tightfisted toward them. Rather, be
openhanded and freely lend them whatever they need.*

Deuteronomy 15:7–8

Former NBA star Dikembe Mutombo is seven feet two and has size 22 feet.

"I've no control over that. The Almighty has plans for us to make a place so we can go on and make a difference," he said. "It all has to do with my faith; I am deeply religious. It goes back to my roots, to my mom and my dad."

Some estimate that he earned more than $100 million while playing with the Denver Nuggets and the Philadelphia 76ers. He didn't blow the dough on fast cars and bling. Instead, he put the money in the bank and decided to give back. (He must know that the fastest way to double your money is to fold it in half and put it back in your wallet.)

He created the Dikembe Mutombo Foundation and built a hospital and research center in the Congo, named after his mom, Biamba. In 1999, his mother had a stroke, just a couple of hours after talking to her son on the phone. Because she couldn't get to a hospital, she died in her living room. He couldn't even attend her funeral because of that nation's civil war. Mutombo donated millions of his own money to create the hospital in honor of his mother and her faith.

"I come from a large family, but I was not raised with a fortune," he said. "Something more was left me, and that was family values."

SWEET FREEDOM IN *Action*

Today, don't listen to liberals when they mock "family values" like they're some relic of an ancient past. Rather, pass them on to your kids and watch what God does to change the world.

JESUS THE GOD-MAN
They gave him a piece of broiled fish,
and he took it and ate it in their presence.
Luke 24:42–43

Here's a math puzzler: how was Jesus 100 percent God and 100 percent man at the same time? It's easy to be overwhelmed by the thought.

But here's a clue: after the most amazing event in history, after being tortured and crucified unto death, only to come back to life, to be resurrected from the dead, Jesus, the Son of God, is what?

He's hungry, and His disciples give Him a piece of boiled fish to eat.

It's easy to read over that line of Scripture and not think about it, or to think it's unimportant. But it's actually super important, because it tells that Jesus, our Lord, God made flesh, was both God and man. He triumphed over death, but He also shared in our earthly concerns, our earthly needs.

There's great comfort in that, because it means God understands everything about you—not just your thoughts and emotions, your sinfulness and your faithfulness. He even knows that you get hungry, that you get thirsty, that you get tired.

God is in the big things of creation, but He's also in every little thing of every day. He's lived as a man has. He knows what it is to be human.

SWEET FREEDOM IN *Action*

Today, reflect on the human side of Jesus and take comfort in the fact that He understands all your needs.

IS GOVERNMENT MAKING YOU FAT?
So whether you eat or drink or whatever you do,
do it all for the glory of God.
1 Corinthians 10:31

Just about everything the government has ever told you about food is wrong. Remember the food pyramid you learned in school? Or even the latest version of it?

Because some bureaucrat created it, it's hung in classrooms all across America. We ate fewer eggs and meats and natural fats, trying to obey their rules. We ate mostly high fructose everything, spiking our insulin and whacking out kids' blood sugar levels, because they told us to. We consumed copious amounts of processed wheat and grain products that are heavily subsidized by the government, because they said it wouldn't get us fat or give us high cholesterol.

And of course the government that authorized drawing up the food pyramid was itself influenced by deep-pocketed lobbyists and pork-barreling politicians.

That food pyramid has been debunked. Americans are fatter now than they've ever been—thanks, food pyramid!—and doctors are handing out drugs like candy to try to control an epidemic of high cholesterol and blood sugar levels. It's staggering to see what happens when government tries to influence every area of your life. America's diet is a good lesson.

Decisions are best made close to home. That's the motto for citizens who believe in self-governance, and there's nothing closer to home than the dinner table. Instead of listening to politicians and faraway bureaucrats for advice on, well, anything...use your own common sense. Do your own research instead of blindly agreeing with a government graph or a politician's wife.

SWEET FREEDOM IN *Action*

When your kids come home with nutrition-class homework, set them straight on that food pyramid, and remind them that your family can be trusted to make good choices.

FLEAS AND OTHER BLESSINGS
Who has known the mind of the Lord?
Or who has been his counselor?
Romans 11:34

One of the first movies I saw was *The Hiding Place*. It changed my life. The movie, a true story, is about Corrie ten Boom and her sister, who were put into the Ravensbruck Nazi concentration camp after they were caught hiding Jews.

Somehow, they managed to sneak in a Bible, which they read repeatedly for comfort and guidance. "Rejoice always, pray constantly, give thanks in all circumstances; for this is the will of God in Christ Jesus," Betsy read aloud. Then she looked around the grimy place and suggested they thank God that she and Corrie were in the same barracks, that the barracks were crowded—so that they could tell more people about Christ—that they had a Bible, and even for the fleas that infested their barracks.

That last part was too much. Corrie emphatically told her sister that even God couldn't make her thankful for disgusting fleas!

The sisters began holding open Bible studies there in the middle of a Nazi concentration camp, leading numerous people to Christ. Mysteriously, the guards never entered their barracks, which meant their Bible studies could go on uninterrupted. And the young women were inexplicably untouched when others around them were assaulted.

Only later did they learn why they were left alone: the guards kept a safe distance from them because they didn't want to get fleas.

SWEET FREEDOM IN *Action*
Today, make a gratitude list . . . and don't leave *anything* off.

BEHOLD THE TURTLE

*Learn to do right; seek justice. Defend the oppressed. Take up
the cause of the fatherless; plead the case of the widow.*
Isaiah 1:17

" **B**ehold the turtle, he makes progress only when he sticks his neck out," said James Bryant Conant.

How often do we overlook injustice because we are too timid to say anything?

Sometimes we are so afraid of hurting someone's feelings that we fail to defend what is right, so nothing gets done about the wrong!

Whether it's a friend who is discriminated against, a family member who should be confronted, or a personal sin that needs to be dealt with—we are constantly faced with opportunities to stand for what is right. But none of these problems can be faced if we act small in timidity.

We can see throughout history that the people who really change the world do so at great personal cost. In fact, our country wouldn't even exist if our Founding Fathers had not been willing to risk the penalty of death to fight against tyranny.

And in the Bible, we see that speaking the Word of God requires courage. Elijah was hunted for three years after daring to stand up to King Ahab. Almost all of the apostles were martyred, but not before Paul had stood before the most powerful man in the world, Caesar, and preached the good news.

SWEET FREEDOM IN *Action*

Today, pray for the Holy Spirit to give you boldness, and look for opportunities to stick your neck out for justice.

HE ALONE SITS ON THE THRONE

But he gives us more grace. That is why Scripture says:
"God opposes the proud but shows favor to the humble."
James 4:6

Many Scripture passages address pride. God must find it needful that we be reminded how He feels about it. Let's just say He doesn't like it. That's mild; God actually HATES a proud look, so says Proverbs 6:17. God's response to the proud is to oppose them. I don't want God opposing me. As a sports fan, I thrive on competition. As a political enthusiast, I think competitive primaries are the best. I understand opposition. And I never want to be God's opponent, trying to muster enough strength—and foolishness—to withstand the Almighty.

But haven't we been taught to have pride in ourselves and our country? To be confident? God's talking about opposing a different sort of pride, as the Merriam-Webster dictionary describes it: "A feeling that you are more important or better than other people." He's got a problem with it because it puts us on the throne of our own lives; it's a form of idolatry where we worship ourselves.

Humility, on the other hand, acknowledges that we owe God everything.

Too often, today's pop culture seems to say: "Be your own God!" Wrong! There is only one God, and He will not be denied.

SWEET FREEDOM IN *Action*

Today, reflect on God's many gifts to you—including the gift of your life—and pray to Him in gratitude and humility.

SLAY THE GRASSHOPPER

All the people we saw there are of great size.... We seemed like
grasshoppers in our own eyes, and we looked the same to them.
Numbers 13:32b–33b

Some people think they're giants; others think they're nothing at all. The former displeases God. The latter doesn't tickle His fancy, either. God can't use a person who plays small and constantly says, "I'm not worthy, Lord," anymore than He can use one who says, "Step aside! I got this, Lord." He wants people who declare, "I can do all this through Him who gives me strength." Translation: "*I can* do this, but only through *You*, Jesus."

If we want to achieve things for God, we need courage, and courage comes from strength. If we belittle ourselves and take a "woe is me" attitude, we send off a weakness vibe that's not going to win any battles. People tend to view you as you view yourself. View yourself as prayer warrior for God.

SWEET FREEDOM IN *Action*

Today, reflect on the true nature of humility. Saying you're a nobody is not the absence of pride; it's the absence of truth, because you are God's creation! Take joy and comfort in that! God knows you can do anything through Him. When you say otherwise, you're saying you know better than God. And that, my friend, is actually just another form of pride. God wants you to be the height of His earthly creation—a faithful man or a faithful woman. Embrace that and serve Him with courage.

A TEEN TEACHES LESSONS IN CONTENTMENT

...fixing our eyes on Jesus, the pioneer and perfecter of faith.
For the joy set before him he endured the cross, scorning its
shame, and sat down at the right hand of the throne of God.
Hebrews 12:2

Jonathan Edwards is best known for his shocking and convicting sermon, "Sinners in the Hands of an Angry God." But, contrary to what you might think, he didn't only preach a fire-and-brimstone message. He gave his first official sermon when he was only eighteen years old, long before he stepped onto the scene in the Great Awakening. It was entitled "Christian Happiness," and it is a strong case for contentment, no matter the situation. This kid's wisdom debuted in 1720 and is still spot-on today!

The young man had a simple and yet beautiful message. It was built with three main points. Christians should be happy because:

1. Our bad things are temporary and will work for our good.
2. Our best things are permanent.
3. Our best times are yet to come.

I can't top that!

SWEET FREEDOM IN *Action*

Today, write Edwards' list on a sticky note and post it on the fridge. Remember, no matter how terrible life seems at the moment, your Heavenly Father is working for your good. Know that the best things you have—God's love and an eternal promise—can never be taken from you. Friends, the best times are still ahead of you!

WHEN TOLERANCE ISN'T TOLERATED
*Be completely humble and gentle; be patient,
bearing with one another in love.*
Ephesians 4:2

Be empowered! Don't accept today's Orwellian definition of "tolerance." It's hijacked verbiage in a society that ignores obvious double standards applied to the culture wars. Your intelligence is underestimated when a pundit ends debate with the accusation of intolerance, merely because a (usually) conservative states something that a liberal doesn't want to consider. It happens every day, all day, on panels of talking heads out-shouting one another on sensitive issues, failing to edify, thus wasting a viewer's time.

Why is this so? Archbishop Charles J. Chaput said, "Evil talks about tolerance only when it's weak. When it gains the upper hand, its vanity always requires the destruction of the good and the innocent, because the example of good and innocent lives is an ongoing witness against it."

In a televised gubernatorial debate, two of my very well-financed, experienced opponents bickered unedifyingly. As any good mom would do, I reprimanded the gentlemen with a reminder that voters deserved better discourse. It was that campaign's turning point that dramatically hushed them so voters could finally hear my own vision. And I won.

True tolerance is listening with patience to what someone else has to say and considering it seriously. But it is not all intolerant to reject falsehood and to stand for God's Truth.

SWEET FREEDOM IN *Action*

Today, pray to treat others with tolerance, to stay firmly planted in God's Word, and to resist pressures to cave and compromise against His law.

HOLIDAY DEVOTIONS

Bringing Peace to the War on Earth

Glory to God in the highest heaven, and on earth
peace to those on whom his favor rests.
Luke 2:14

Christmas—with its message of hope, peace, joy, and the fellowship of mankind—is a holiday for everyone. So isn't it amazing that every year we hear more accounts of a ramped-up "war on Christmas"?

How sad that a handful of grinches are at war with the annual celebration of the birth of the Christ, whose coming was prophesied centuries earlier and was then gloriously heralded by the angels with a blessing for "peace on earth." Even if they don't believe the story, it's a shame they can't at least recognize the beauty of the message. Can't they let everyone else enjoy the season without throwing a temper tantrum at the sight of a Nativity scene? People who feel affronted by a baby in a humble manger display or a few Christmas carols have lost all sense of proportion and really seem in need of holiday cheer.

At a time when our country is divided on so many things, Christmas unites us. It is a needed reminder that although the Enemy tries to pit us against each other, our Savior came to earth as a lowly baby to restore peace to our fallen world.

Sweet Freedom in *Action*

So in this Advent season, let's shout a cheery "Merry Christmas" to everyone we meet. Let's be the embodiment of the peace and hope Jesus brought when He entered the world over two thousand years ago.

TREKKING TO BETHLEHEM
Where is the one who has been born king of the Jews?
We saw his star when it rose and have come to worship him.
Matthew 2:2

A merica is at a crossroads. The values of our nation are hanging in the
balance. The culture is proclaiming that up is down and down is up.
Traditional American values are frequently mocked in the public square.
Even many of our politicians in Washington reject the ultimate truth upon
which our Founders built this great nation.

In the midst of such tumultuous times, it is even more important than
ever that we study the story of the magi this Christmas. The Wise Men
from the East received a message of Jesus's birth. They put aside everything
else in their lives to find the Messiah and worship Him. They trekked to
Bethlehem in search of answers. There, they found Jesus. They honored
Him.

The story of the Wise Men reminds us that it's wise to go after Him,
to seek Him, to pursue knowledge of Him. This is even more imperative
as our culture turns from the Truth.

SWEET FREEDOM IN

This Christmas let's reread Matthew 2 and choose to be like the Wise
Men. Make your own "trek to Bethlehem" by putting Him before everything else in your life. May this season give you a glimpse of the
faith that compelled the wisest men 2000 years ago...and may we all
be given great wisdom as well!

CHRISTMAS IS A STATE OF MIND

For to us a child is born, to us a son is given, and the
government will be on his shoulders. And he will be called
Wonderful Counselor, Mighty God, Everlasting Father,
Prince of Peace.
Isaiah 9:6

Ronald Reagan said Christmas was a "state of mind. It is found throughout the year whenever faith overcomes doubt, hope conquers despair, and love triumphs over hate." This Christmas season, let's be thankful that we live in a country known for striving to embody these values. And let's be grateful for the brave men and women in uniform who have fought to defend our values and who may be spending this Christmas far from home.

During seasons of sharing with family and friends, Todd and I love spending time with our large, diverse family, gratefully acknowledging God's blessings, and trying to spread those blessings around. But for many people, Christmas is a lonely time. Maybe their loved one is serving overseas in the military, maybe someone close to them recently died, maybe they don't have a family to call their own. They need our touch. The greatest gift we can give this season is to honor our Savior by showing those around us His unending love!

SWEET FREEDOM IN *Action*

This Christmas, will you invite someone who is struggling or is lonely to join in your festivities? As Christians we should always make room at the table for those who may be hurting, especially on the day we celebrate the birth of Jesus, who came to save the *whole* world. His love will shine through you this season.

HOPE IN THINGS ETERNAL
But now, Lord, what do I look for? My hope is in you.
Psalm 39:7

Easter is the celebration of what ultimate hope really means. In Jesus's triumph over death through His Resurrection, death was defeated and hope became the expectation of eternal life with God.

Hope is the great driving force in many of our lives, and it has been the driving force in our country's history. America has always had a strong sense that God's Providence is abundant, that no challenge can ever be too great and no enemy too strong. It was this hope that inspired us to carve a nation out of the wilderness, to appreciate opportunities to responsibly utilize nature's resources, to engineer skyscrapers towering over our gleaming cities, and to fly to the moon.

As a country and as individuals, we can always have true hope to guide us. Put your faith in that, not in man. The world and its leaders will always come up short; people will disappoint us; governments will never be able to meet our needs. But if we look to our Savior to lead us, we will find answers and our hope will be proven and strengthened.

It is from that solid hope that we can truly help our fellow man and help lead our government back toward the only One who can redeem us.

SWEET FREEDOM IN *Action*

This Easter, remember our Lord's sacrifice that led to the Resurrection, and don't keep the joy of the day inside! Find helpful, practical ways to share what you know about Jesus's sacrifice.

Honoring Our Men and Women in Uniform
Be on your guard; stand firm in the faith;
be courageous; be strong.
1 Corinthians 16:13

I proudly display a bumper sticker that proclaims: "If you love your freedom, thank a vet!" It was on the 11th hour of the 11th day of the 11th month of 1918 that the armistice between Germany and the Allied nations ended World War One. A year later the White House commemorated the day as one to be "filled with solemn pride in the heroism of those who died in the country's service and with gratitude for the victory." Years later 11/11 was officially declared Veterans Day.

We are thankful for this day being set aside to remember our veterans, and many of us are overwhelmed with pride and respect for those we honor today. America's men and women in uniform selflessly sacrificed—some giving all—to protect the freedom and opportunities we enjoy today. They are the embodiment of 1 Corinthians 16:13!

Sweet Freedom in *Action*

In honor of everything our veterans have given, please remember them and thank them in tangible ways. Be creative in this. If nearby, visit a veterans' hospital and deliver flowers or treats. Help the widow of a veteran with chores around her house. Help with community events that honor vets. Show your pride in their efforts to keep us free by displaying our beautiful American flag! May God bless, protect, and heal the hurts of America's finest. God bless our veterans.

THE CITY UPON THE HILL
Let us come before him with thanksgiving
and extol him with music and song.
Psalm 95:2

Four hundred years ago a courageous group of men and women fleeing religious persecution set a new course for human history in a new frontier. Those early pioneers landed upon a rocky shoreline and set about establishing their new life. Centuries later, America sets the example of what can come from a free and hardworking people. We are the shining city upon a hill that the colonial leader John Winthrop implored us to be.

What started as a small colony grew into the most exceptional nation in history. We have so much to be thankful for! God's mercy and grace and His hand of protection granted us this exceptionalism. Be grateful. He trusted us with rich natural food and energy resources, fertile land, foundations for beautiful cities, and the talented and industrious people we call "our fellow Americans." We pray that God will continue to bless America.

In his farewell address, President Reagan reminded us that "all great change in America begins at the dinner table." The Thanksgiving season—traditionally centered around an overflowing table—can be a time of collective contemplation about where we are as a nation and where we should be in order to remain prosperous and free. Take time to discuss these things with each other, especially the young people in your family. They may not be taught in school the truth about our nation's foundation and her history—so you do the teaching. At Thanksgiving dinner our family goes around the table with mandatory participation in "I am thankful for.... " This year I'm adding to it, no matter how many eyes will roll when I give the instructions. Everyone will be asked to think of ways our nation can be better and more deserving of blessings. Before the first bite of mashed potatoes, I want to hear what each individual plans to do about it.

SWEET FREEDOM IN *Action*

Today, offer up prayers of happy thanksgiving for God's great blessings to our exceptional nation—and let's pray to make America better and more worthy of God's favor.

IN GOD WE TRUST

Do not put your trust in princes, in human beings, who cannot save. When their spirit departs, they return to the ground; on that very day their plans come to nothing. Blessed are those whose help is the God of Jacob, whose hope is in the Lord their God. He is the Maker of heaven and earth, the sea, and everything in them—he remains faithful forever. He upholds the cause of the oppressed and gives food to the hungry.
Psalm 146:3–7

The United States of America is a wonderful country, but sometimes, politics can be depressing. We can work so hard to elect honorable people to Washington, D.C., only for them to disappoint us when they get there. We can work together to solve a societal problem, only to see government policies hamper our progress. We can believe with all our hearts that *this time* a new leader and a new agenda will save us, but alas, no human can save the world.

Thank God, God already has! And He will never fail us. Nations rise and fall, kings come and go, but our Lord will always sit upon His throne. His touch is the only thing that can truly free the oppressed, heal the brokenhearted, protect us from enemies, and give hope for a better tomorrow.

SWEET FREEDOM IN *Action*

This Presidents' Day, thank God for the good leaders He's given us. And when politicians inevitably disappoint with blunders and broken campaign promises, hold them accountable while resting in the knowledge that our Father is the King above all kings and in Him alone we will put our trust. He will never break a promise.

For Those Who Paid the Ultimate Price

Greater love has no one than this:
to lay down one's life for one's friends.
John 15:13

Take a moment to soberly consider that people have died to protect our basic rights. Freedom's cost is so high and its value is so great that we should honor our veterans above any celebrity, athlete, or politician. All of us who love freedom need to be willing to protect it and to honor those who have fought for it.

On days like this, it's easy to encourage others to think of Christ. Freedom is so precious, *we are so precious*, that God Himself laid down His life to set us free.

We have a responsibility to use this incredible gift called freedom wisely. Paul gives us instructions in Galatians 5:13–14: "You, my brothers, were called to be free. But do not use your freedom to indulge the flesh; rather, serve one another humbly in love. For the entire law is fulfilled in keeping this one command: 'Love your neighbor as yourself.'"

Do you see the close relationship between liberty and love? American soldiers' love of country has given us earthly freedom. And even greater— much greater—the sacrifice of Jesus Christ was the greatest act of love the world has ever seen: it set us free from sin; it offers us eternal life. We have merely to accept that gift.

Sweet Freedom in *Action*

This Memorial Day, thank God for freedom. Pray for the courage to defend it. Support our veterans and active-duty troops in tangible ways— let them know you care.

Most Important Job on the Planet

For I am the Lord your God who takes hold of your
right hand and says to you, Do not fear; I will help you.

Isaiah 41:13

The greatest privilege of my life has been being a mom. It was because of my love for my children and concern for their future that I entered politics. I would do anything to ensure they grow up in the same great land of the free that I did.

When I began to see ideologies opposed to freedom creeping in to our community, the mama grizzly in me came roaring out and made me say, "Wait a minute!" Armed with a relentless love for children, I entered the arena to protect their futures by protecting Alaska's future—and America's future.

Of course there are challenges, but when self-doubt whispers in my ear, I am reminded that God hadn't asked me to be a perfect politician or a perfect mom. He doesn't demand that I have all the answers. He only asks that I show up everyday ready to love my country and love my children and point them toward Him. He will give me the strength to get through the hard days, and He will never forsake us. He alone sustains us.

Sweet Freedom in *Action*

So to all you other mama grizzlies out there, remember as you're tempted to lie awake at night anxious about the next generation's future, they're resting in the most secure place—the palm of our Heavenly Father. He takes their hands, and ours, promising He'll never let go.

THE NATURAL RESOURCE WE NEED TO RENEW
Whoever fears the Lord has a secure fortress,
and for their children it will be a refuge.
Proverbs 14:26

I've always enjoyed watching Todd in his role as "dad." When I married him, I knew he was a good man, but watching him father our five children reveals an even greater depth of character. From coaching the kids on how to play sports, to teaching them to love and respect our wild Alaskan frontier, to instilling in them virtue and a hunger for justice, I am so thankful for the loving father that he is.

Not everyone has been fortunate enough to grow up with a good father—some, unfortunately, grow up without a father around at all. It's tragic but true that kids who grow up without a father can have a tougher time understanding what a good and loving father should be. Churches need to do all they can to reach out to single mothers and help them. One way is through children's and teen's Bible study that emphasizes biblical examples of what it means to be a good man or woman. Just as important, they need to be shown what a true, loving, and eternal Father we have in God.

SWEET FREEDOM IN *Action*

Today, enjoy to the hilt the celebration of dads who strive to be the strong and loving fathers God has called them to be. Our world desperately needs good fathers whose actions ultimately reflect our Heavenly Father's love for His creation and all peoples. The one natural resource that we're most in need of replenishing is good fatherhood. Let's pray for ways we can help prepare the next generation of great dads.

CELEBRATING TRUE FREEDOM
It is for freedom that Christ has set us free.
Stand firm, then, and do not let yourselves be burdened again
by a yoke of slavery.
Galatians 5:1

Independence Day is a climactic summer celebration where we hone in on all the freedoms we enjoy as Americans. It's great fun! But we must also never forget that the freedom that we celebrate came from and has been preserved through sacrifice. Our Founding Fathers and the many patriots who came after them understood how precious it is to live as free men and women. Many have paid the ultimate price by giving their lives to ensure that all Americans who came after them would also live in freedom.

There is a saying that sometimes accompanies pictures of American soldiers: "Some people wake up, stretch, and enjoy freedom. Some people wake up, stretch, and defend it."

We should never take freedom for granted. We should always respect those who defend our freedom. And we must pass our love for freedom, and our desire to protect it, to our children. We have to be the patriots that our nation needs and can call on.

If we are to remain an exceptional nation, if we are to remain a beacon to the world, if we are going to successfully perpetuate freedom for future generations of Americans, we have to resolve here and now to take action in our neighborhoods, our communities, our cities, our counties, and our states, and pray that our country remains one nation under God, with liberty and freedom for all. That is what we celebrate today—the fight to ensure every human being has the ability to live free, as God intends.

SWEET FREEDOM IN *Action*

Today, enjoy the fireworks and the lemonade and the hot dogs and potato salad, and resolve that tomorrow—and the rest of the year—you will be active in work to keep America great.

ACKNOWLEDGMENTS

Proof that God is still in the miracle-working business: after decades of contemplation and journaling insights, this book is finally wrapped up and now presented to those who'll look outside of self to find sweet freedom. Thank you, Lord! Thank you for answering.

Besides the Rock upon which I must stand or I'll sink, I acknowledge my family and friends who hold up one another's right arm, so as helpmates we all may accomplish much.

Todd, for your patience through another sometimes arduous process, thank you for constantly picking up the slack and never putting your own self in front of leading this family. For my kids and their kids because they're the lights of my life! Track, Bristol, Willow, Piper, Trig, Tripp, Kyla, and new baby girl—I love you more than life itself. Mom, Dad, Chuck, Heather, Molly, and your fantastic families; all our in-laws; the entire extended tribe including Karen (because Trig hollers for YOU more than for me!), I love you all.

And there's more earthly help I'm proud to acknowledge and proclaim how honored I am to work with, starting with Robert Barnett—the country's sharpest, most conscientious attorney. To the fun and flawless team at Regnery Publishing that will soon take over the book world because you're in it for the right reasons—including Marji Ross, publisher; Bob DeMoss, editor in chief of Regnery Faith; Harry Crocker, Katharine Spence, and the rest of the fantastic editorial team; John Caruso and Jason Sunde for their work on the book cover and design; Mark Bloomfield and the sales and marketing team; Patricia Jackson and Alyssa Cordova, publicity; and everyone else there at their D.C. office—I couldn't have done this without YOUR hard work and that extra sweet incentive greeting me in your office—next time I'll bake the best for all of YOU!

A most sincere thank-you to Nancy and Camille French—your constant positive vibe flowed through the airwaves and keyboard clicks—AGAIN—writing THIS book! The French family encourages the country because they're smart, kind, selfless, and humble. Nancy—I've never met a woman like you who really does it all and remains so grounded—deflecting any praise as you give all the glory to God. (It's why He'll keep overflowing your cup, my friend!) This book came together because of YOU.

My deepest appreciation for Team Palin—our very small but very impacting motley crew that certainly has more mirthful enjoyment behind the political scene than anyone has a right to. Seriously, your A-Team, varsity abilities, work ethic, loyalty, and humor have driven our mission forward since the day we met on the vice presidential trail. You are the best. Keep inspired by remembering the life-changing influence you have throughout the United States, specifically over good people like Lisa and Jonathan. We have years ahead of us, together, knowing the plans for this team are for GOOD.

Finally, it's the continued covering provided by Prayer Warriors across the world that allows me to stand upon the Rock. Without you creating a shield I'd be toast. Please keep the prayers flowing and our nation will be better for it. I pray for you, too—that you and your families will be so blessed, and that you'll see your prayers answered. Adrienne, Deann, Deb, Juanita, Kelsey, Kim, Kristie, Lori, Mary, Pam…and so many more—your input shared after constant meditation on God's big picture is in this book. It's you, too, speaking to the world on these pages. Thank you.

NOTES

NOTES

NOTES

NOTES

NOTES

NOTES

NOTES

NOTES

NOTES